ART
OF
ENTREPRENEURS

Copyright

Art of Entrepreneurs:
Discover Your Creative Genius
By Brad Ball

Published by:

Ardent Creative
550 Reserve Street #190, Southlake, TX 76092
www.ardentcreative.com

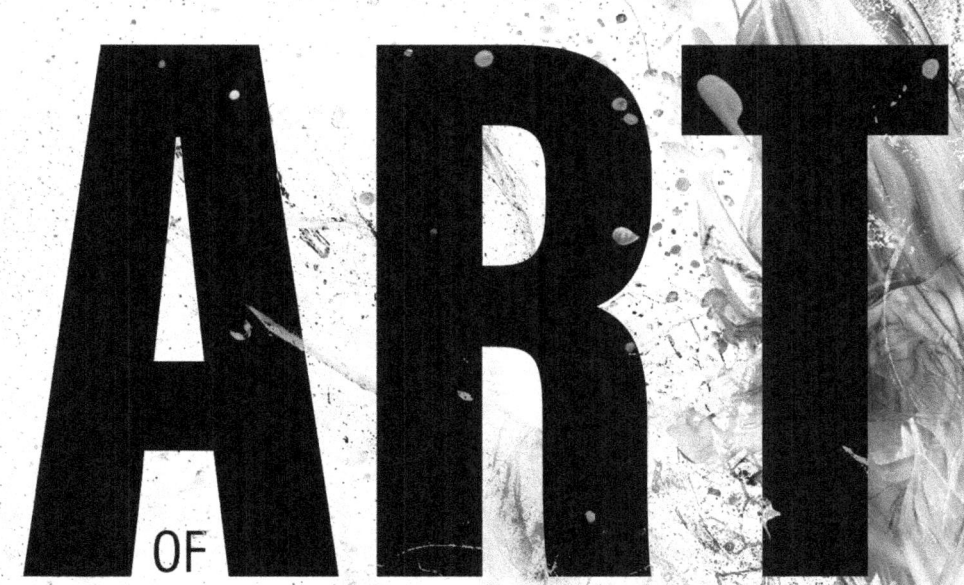

ART
OF
ENTREPRENEURS

DISCOVER YOUR CREATIVE GENIUS

BRAD BALL

Table of Contents

Acknowledgements

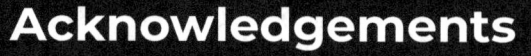

Writing this book has been an incredible journey, and I am deeply grateful to all who have supported me along the way. If you told me ten years ago I would have written a book, I would have said, "You're crazy. I'm an artist, not a writer."

First, thank you to my Lord and Savior Jesus Christ. Through him, all things are possible, and he deserves all the credit for the good he has made of me today.

Next, thank you to my wife Leah for her unwavering support, patience, and love, who has been my sure foundation throughout this process. To my children, Tanner, Tori and Madi, thank you for your understanding during the long hours and for constantly inspiring me to see the world through fresh eyes. Each of you are extremely creative and will continue to share this legacy on your own journeys.

To my dad, Frank Ball, thank you for instilling in me the values of hard work, creativity, and perseverance that have shaped much of who I am today. Also, a major thanks for taking my word vomit and helping turn it into a book we can both be proud of. I am proud to work with you but even more so to call you Dad.

To my brothers, Mark and Chris, thanks for beating me up as a kid so I knew I could do hard things. Big thanks, Mark, for taking on our Verity software project and seeing it through to the end.

I am profoundly grateful to my team at Ardent Creative. Your dedication, creativity, and support have not only made our company thrive, but you have also given me the freedom to pursue this project. Special thanks to my business partner, David Canington, for all of your support and for challenging me to become the best version of myself—and also for sticking with it for the last twenty years. To Paul Miller, thank you for your creative encouragement and inspiring me on this journey. James, Jay, and Anna, you rock, and I love all the years we have worked together.

To my partners and fellow entrepreneurs in the Committed Mastermind and War Room, your insights, challenges, and encouragement have been invaluable. JC and Karen Hite, your friendship and mentorship have been crucial in my entrepreneurial journey. Vinnie Fisher, you have been a wonderful example of what Godly leadership in business is all about. Tony Grebmeier, your constant encouragement and support inspired me on this journey beyond my comfort zone. Ryan Deiss, Roland Fraser, Deanna Rogers, and Perry Belcher—my days in the War Room Mastermind started this journey. Sending out a weekly email inspiring your employees is where it all started, and recognition of that need began in your room.

Thank you, Mark de Grasse, the first to read my manuscript and give me valuable feedback.

My gratitude to Trevor Crane and Tracy Brown for their expert guidance in shaping this book. Your insights and attention to detail have been instrumental in bringing this vision to life.

Thank you, Ken Moskowitz, for your detailed feedback and encouragement, which has inspired me to make this book so much better than what it was in the beginning. You truly are one of the best copywriters and editors in the world.

Oliver Graf and Sam Khorramian, your creativity and art inspires me. Your ability to impact real estate is a perfect example of how art can impact business. Thanks for our random painting days and allowing me to use our awesome crown painting.

To my clients, past and present, thank you for trusting me with your projects and for being a constant source of inspiration. Your challenges and successes have taught me more than you know. To all the artists, entrepreneurs, and dreamers who have shared their stories with me over the years—your passion and creativity have fueled my journey and inspired many of the ideas in this book.

Lastly, to my mom. You always believed in me, even when I didn't. You have been in Heaven for a long time but your light is always inspiring me to believe in myself. Thank you for always leading me and guiding me on this journey of life.

This book is a testament to the power of creativity and collaboration. Thank you all for being part of this adventure.

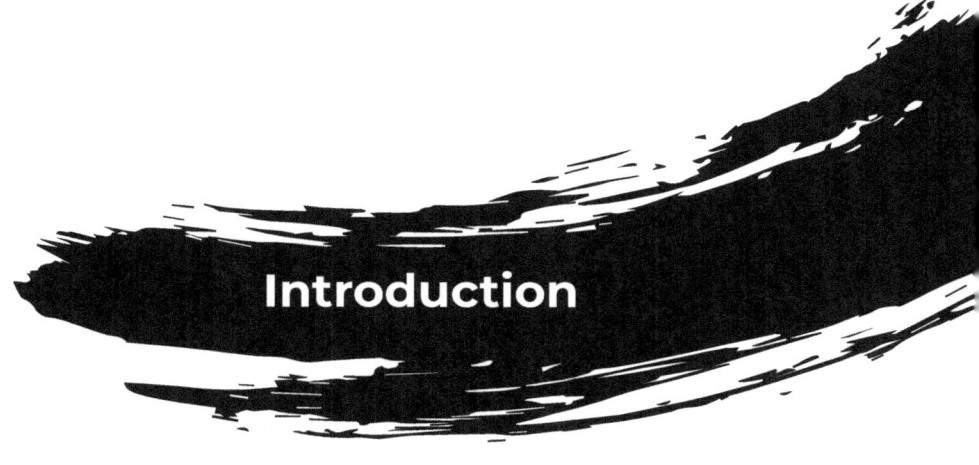

Introduction

Welcome to the dawn of a fresh creative awakening—a powerful catalyst to unlock the limitless reservoir of creativity within you. Creativity is more than a spark. It's a lasting flame that, once ignited, can illuminate your mind and transform your entrepreneurial journey.

As you begin this journey, remember that creativity isn't a destination but is an ongoing adventure—a process of discovery and reinvention that will transform how you see challenges and opportunities in both business and everyday life.

By the end of this book, you will have simple strategies to apply creativity to your everyday life, overcome creative blocks, and embrace innovation through an ARTistic mindset.

Creativity, innovation, and invention have existed since stone hammers and paintings on cave walls. If you are a business leader or anyone who is thinking, *I am not creative*, then this book is especially for you. If you already embrace your creative side, this book will help you dive deeper into the process.

No matter your age or position in business, creativity is the bedrock of growth and success. From the initial steps of this journey to each milestone along the way, this book will help cultivate creativity within, transform the raw material of the mind, and provide powerful tools to enhance your life.

A new wave of creativity can lead to groundbreaking innovations in your organization. Picture awakening a long-dormant part of yourself that holds the key to your success. Envision a fresh perspective that allows you to solve problems you once thought insurmountable.

From the earliest cave paintings to the latest technological advancements, creativity is the spark that has driven us forward. It's the same mother of invention that led to the creation of the wheel, the building of the pyramids, and the exploration of space. Yet despite its importance, many people think creativity is a rare gift bestowed upon a lucky few. They would be wrong. It doesn't matter who you are, where you come from, or what you think about yourself, you can become a creative genius.

Creativity is not confined to the arts or to those who call themselves "artists." It's not just about painting, writing, or composing music. It's about problem-solving, innovative thinking, and the ability to see connections where others don't take time to notice. It's about imagining new possibilities and having the courage to pursue them.

Remember how companies like Uber, Airbnb or Netflix transformed their industries. Each of the businesses weren't artistic by nature, but they required the vision to see past the current way of doing things. They created a better solution that is consumed now more than anyone could've imagined. The more you stand outside the box, the more impact it will have on everything inside and outside of the box.

Think about the last time you solved a problem at work, came up with a new way to organize your home, or thought of a fun activity for your family. Those are examples of using creativity in action—not a rare talent but a natural part of everyday life.

This book provides tools, techniques, and exercises to help you unlock your creative potential. Learn how to overcome mental blocks and fears that hold you back. Discover how to cultivate a creative mindset and integrate creativity into everyday life.

The creative journey can bring joy, fulfillment, and a sense of purpose. It can open doors to unbelievable opportunities and take you where others never thought to go.

Now is your chance to spark creative ability that has been dormant since childhood. Enjoy relationships that flourish because of your unique way of thinking, a life filled with excitement and curiosity. This book is about helping you become the best version of yourself.

In a world that is constantly changing at an ever-increasing pace, the ability to think creatively is more important than ever. It's the key to staying relevant and competitive, to adapting and thriving in the face of increasing competition. It will set you apart in a crowded marketplace and will drive your success.

So whether you are young or old, whether you see yourself as creative or not, this book is for you. There is no better time than now to unlock your creative potential and transform your future.

As an artist and entrepreneur, I have always put the expression of art at the forefront of my life. My passion is to see clients succeed, not to get rich, receive awards, or earn accolades. For me, a job well done is always the best form of recognition.

Great work speaks for itself. Ardent Creative has received many awards. As an artist, I won scholarships and art awards throughout college. My art has been seen worldwide, published in international books, and used in presentations, traveling as far away as Paraguay. As one of the first live "speed" painters, I have painted before tens of thousands. As a designer, I have over thirty years of experience working with companies like American Airlines, Samsung, Higginbotham, Alcon, and the Gladney Center for Adoption. None of that could have happened without the release of some God-given creativity.

From one artist to another, welcome to the beginning of your creative journey. Let's embark on it together and see where it leads.

The Blank
Canvas

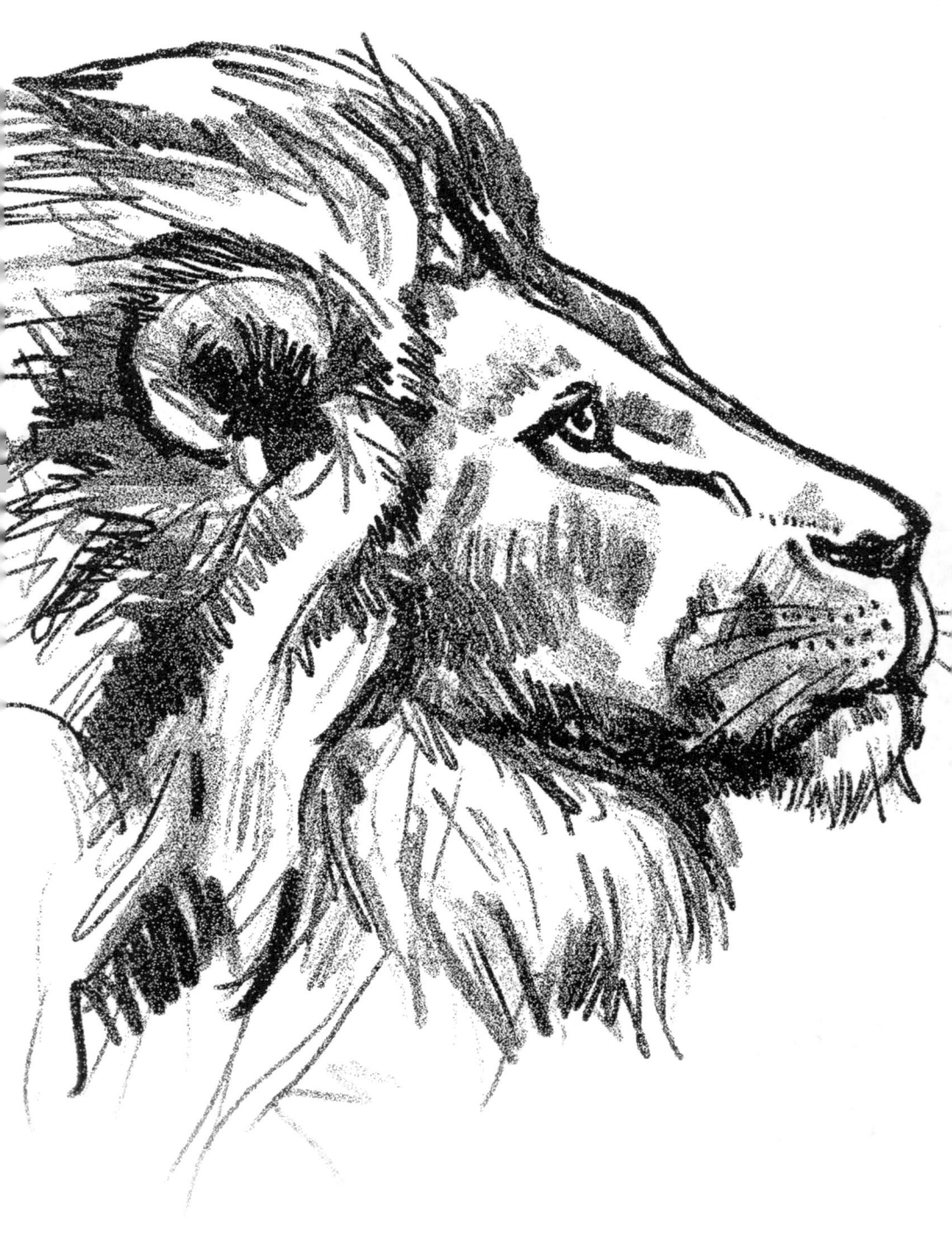

An Artist's Beginning Sketches

Art transcends the mere act of putting pencil to paper, brush to canvas, or fingers to strings. It's an outpouring of the soul, a manifestation of our thoughts and emotions. True art resonates deep within, stirring a maelstrom of passion and intensity that can only find its voice through creative expression.

In the realm of entrepreneurship, this artistic approach becomes a powerful tool for innovation and problem-solving, allowing us to paint our visions on the canvas of the business world with bold strokes of daring ingenuity.

Being an entrepreneur is more than ink on a page. Like a symphony, hundreds of strings are plucked for the notes to be played. If one note is wrong or the timing is off, you'll notice. The conductor's leadership is essential to keep everyone in sync. You may be the conductor, a cellist, or maybe a percussionist, but whatever your position is, you are an essential part to complete the symphony.

Ideas and beauty happen in the sketches. As business leaders, customers may only see the end product, but every product started as an idea, "a beginning sketch." We've all heard a "napkin" story. You might even have one yourself. It's that moment when you have a big idea but nothing is handy to write it down on. Frantically, you search for anything to capture the thought. A simple restaurant napkin became the life-changing helper. It's basic, but it gets the job done. Quickly, the idea is jotted down, documented, and saved from slipping away.

My good friend Ryan Deiss has a such a story. Early in his entrepreneurial journey, he was riding the highs and lows of e-commerce and marketing when inspiration struck. At that moment, all he had was a pen and a napkin. That simple idea scribbled on a napkin became revolutionary—the foundation of everything he's built over the last twenty-five years: his first Marketing Funnel.

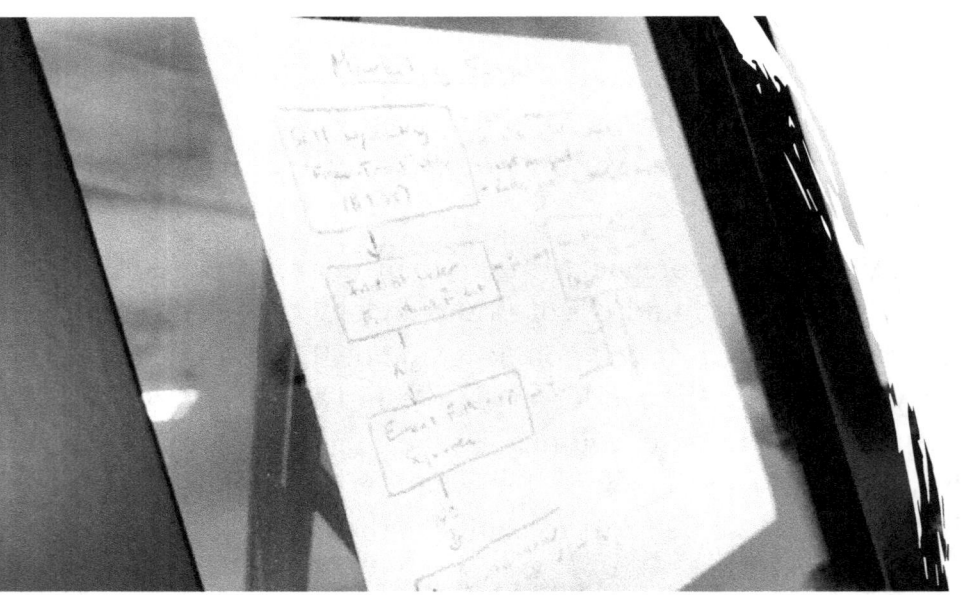

This napkin charts a customer's path on the journey from lead to customer, and several steps in between. If the customer said no, they went one way. But if they said yes, a different path was taken, all leading to one thing—becoming a customer.

An Artist's Beginning Sketches

From this one napkin came an even greater spark of brand awareness to becoming a loyal advocate. It's a similar roadmap, guiding businesses through the crucial steps of attracting, converting, and retaining customers by strategically moving them through the stages of the ascension ladder: **Awareness, Engagement, Subscribe, Convert, Excite, Ascend, Advocate,** and **Promote**.

What started as a few words—lines and squares on a napkin—has since evolved into a guiding light for thousands of businesses. In these creative moments, ideas scratched onto paper come alive, and we find the spark to build something beyond what we ever imagined.

We all need "napkins" in our businesses and teams to turn ideas into realities. Your leadership, directing with vision and passion, is essential for success. With vision, you can orchestrate a plan (the symphony), place the most qualified players in lead positions (section leads), and encourage creativity to zig when others might take the traditional zag. Without a creative mindset, you might still succeed, but the venture will be more difficult and more likely to fail.

An artist is inside everyone, including you, ready and waiting to be released. Now is the time to be inspired and unlock the creative genius you already have but hasn't yet been fully revealed. Awaken it, if you will. Maybe you're like many people who think they aren't creative. Either way, get ready for exciting discoveries about yourself. Let this book be a springboard to launch you into spectacular levels of creativity. As we move from the blank canvas to sketching your entrepreneurial blueprint, remember that every brushstroke counts.

Creativity brings everything to life in vibrant color. Our society with no artistic expression would be living in a boring, black-and-white world where something new is seldom considered. Everything stays the same. Improvements are rare. Life gets better and better because of so many innovations, colors, and designs. New ideas are priceless. Even the bad ideas are good because they encourage something better.

The most widespread and easily accepted forms of artistic expression today are music and theater. For music, the words and melodies create an emotional response. Simply put, we are *moved*. A song not heard for twenty years is immediately recalled upon hearing the first few notes. A play or piece of art can open the door to treasured memories.

In business, creativity and art are often left for the marketing department. "They are the creative people," an owner might say. There is no better time than now for business leaders to see themselves with fresh potential for creative genius. Without creativity there is no worthwhile vision. We just become copycats. For starters, leading people requires creativity because everybody is different. The *worst* we can do is treat everybody exactly the same. Our creativity allows us to handle the unexpected, and doesn't the unexpected happen to us all the time? Without creativity, a business might coast, but it can't forge ahead.

I would like to challenge all leaders and all who would like to better themselves to open your imaginations to an amazing new world of possibility. It's been said that by the time we graduate grade school, most of our creativity has been trained out of us. We've been misled to believe success comes from being like everybody else who is successful.

It's time for business leaders to dare to be different—to grow their passions, improve their business environments, and enjoy better times among family and friends at home. So what is holding you back?

Exercise: On a sheet of paper, even a napkin, write down five past failures. Next, assess whether they are truly over. Could they be adapted into something new? Then identify the difficulty of seeing it come to fruition.

Fear to Start

Fear is a formidable foe, so much so that for many, we're afraid to even start. Worrying about what people might think can be a passion killer. You may love music but are afraid people will judge you. You love art, but struggle because you judge yourself harshly. Fear is a destruction of the mind, creativity, and all that is worth striving for.

In opposition to fear, we must find courage. The first time I painted at a live event, I was terrified. Stepping out and doing something no one had ever done was overwhelming. I could have let fear hold me back, but I took a deep breath and stepped out on the stage with only my creativity and paints. Was this going to work? I'd never know if I didn't give it my best effort. In the span of an hour, I had painted something to be proud of. The central focus of the painting was a candle, which symbolized the light in our lives and how one small light can illuminate a large room. Where there is light, the path can become clear and can eliminate our inner fear and trembling.

In the movie *The Wizard of Oz*, the main character, Dorothy, isn't in Kansas anymore. The Scarecrow, the Tin Man, and the Lion are important influences in her walk down The Yellow Brick Road. The Scarecrow didn't have a brain. The Tin Man lacked a heart. And the Lion had no courage. Fear held each character back, making it impossible to reach their true potential.

Fear makes it almost impossible for us to become successful entrepreneurs. On our road to success, we must overcome our liabilities but learn the value of having an effective team. That is what Dorothy and company were—a team. Each one's strength was a value to the whole. Together, they achieved success.

It's not a question of whether we are smart enough or if our ideas are good enough. Do we have the heart and determination to learn from our failures and never give up?

With fear, will you stop short of the breakthrough that could propel you over the next hill to success? Letting such questions motivate you is an important key to success. Everybody is good at something, provided they conquer their fears and refuse to quit.

Exercise: Identify three key areas where your fears have held you back. Reflect on how you might overcome or sidestep those fears. Then, let your fears be known and ask for help.

Begin with a Stroke

Every journey begins with an important first step, which is overcoming the fear to start. After that comes the passion and courage to persevere through any obstacle. When I pick up a brush, I don't always know where I am going to start. But I have to start somewhere. With the brush in hand, I dab into the most brilliant blue. With precision, I drag the brush from the top of the canvas and make a random stroke. No one knows what the painting will be, and I am the only who to know what will come next. One stroke leads to the next. One step leads to the next.

I was asked last-minute to paint for a concert in front of 3,000 students. With no ideas, I set up on a seven-foot-high platform, grabbed a brush, and made the first stroke across the canvas. Not knowing what I was going to do or where I was going, I stepped back to process what I could create from this randomness. My emotions were high. Fear and the thought of being an on-stage failure set in. However, instead of letting fear take control, I pushed myself toward a solution. I paused. Could I see what wasn't yet there? I saw the foundation of what I could turn into a lion. Boom! With a clear image in my mind, I could focus on what needed to happen next. I reworked the paint, adding the nose, eyes, and mouth. In minutes, a random splatter of paint turned it into a lion masterpiece.

The entrepreneurial journey is much the same. The excitement for what an enterprise might become is an even greater thrill than a painter's first brushstroke on a canvas. With just one spark of an idea, taking a step back to view the scenario, then finding vision and purpose, that first step can turn into something wonderful.

You might be thinking, *I'm not an artist. I can't even draw a stick figure.* Okay, if you say so. But I'm thinking you can. Nobody said your stick figure had to be perfect. Can you draw a circle? Yes. Okay, can you draw a line? Yes. Then guess what? That's all there is to drawing a stick figure. Just put together the circles and lines. You really can do it. And if you do, it will be your own special work of art, unlike what others would draw.

In chess, the first move is so simple, one might think it's insignificant. An artist knows otherwise. It has to anticipate the obstacles ahead and how the game might play out. Strategy requires anticipation of all that might go right or wrong, playing to the strengths and weaknesses presented with each move. The artist must imagine beyond the obvious, looking for a creative move that the casual observer would never anticipate.

From where you are right now, what's your next move? What if you went the other way, doing just the opposite? The clock is ticking. You must decide, but just a second can present several possibilities that would otherwise be missed. With those considerations, you can proceed with greater confidence. An old biblical truism says people without a vision will perish. That's true for business ventures too. If you don't know where you're headed and the best next steps to get you there, you could wind up anywhere.

An Artist's Beginning Sketches

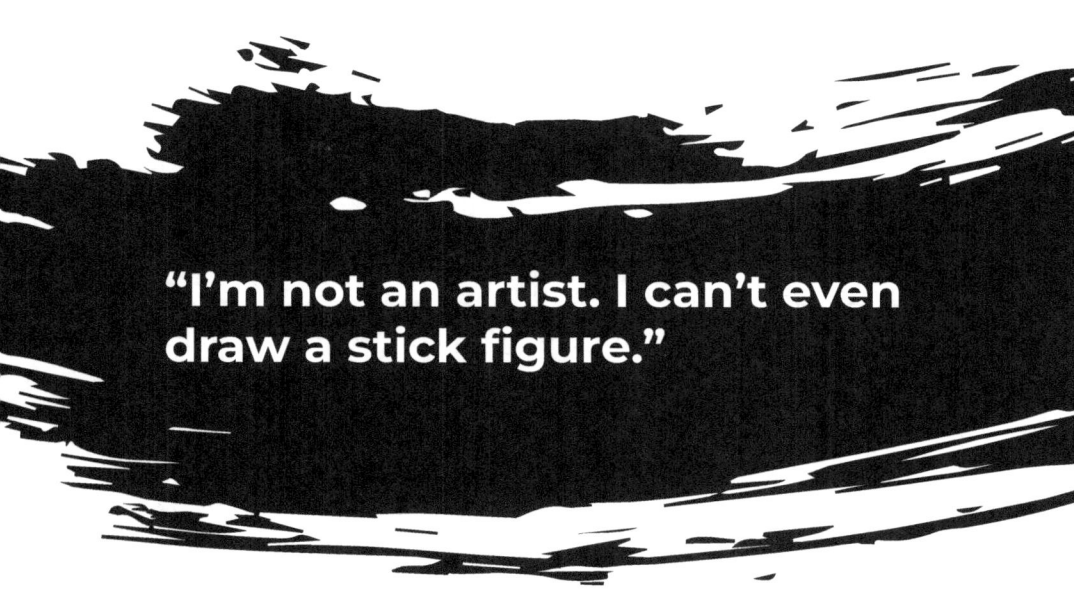

"I'm not an artist. I can't even draw a stick figure."

In moving forward, I find it most helpful to remember where we've been, considering both our failures and our successes. What have we accomplished? What went wrong? What went right? Make a list. Often the very thing that was an asset was also a liability. Why is this important? Without such questions, we deprive ourselves of the crucial lessons that would contribute to our future success.

Failures can be one of our greatest teachers, as long as we don't allow them to stifle our creativity. Use your mistakes as steppingstones, not stumbling blocks. Don't overlook them as something past that doesn't matter. Anticipate failure and strive to avoid it, but never *fear* it. An essential part of your vision for success will come from learning what *not* to do.

I've been told to plan our work and work our plan. As we anticipate the future, we must draw our roadmap that sets clear goals and milestones to mark achievements along the way. There is a potential problem here, because the more time we spend planning our journey, the less time we have to find out if our ideas will work. If we're not careful, we can invest so much in our plan that we're compelled to keep investing more and more to guarantee the success of something that will never work. Instead, I like to test an idea's merit as soon as possible, with as little expense as possible, so we can see the pitfalls we would have missed and build momentum toward what works best.

I heard someone say, "if you want to get to the moon, don't set that as your goal. Shoot for the sun because you will achieve far more than you ever could imagine by just shooting for the moon." Of course, this points to the BHAG, the Big Hairy Audacious Goal, but it's much more than that. It also says that (1) we don't want to limit our possibilities and (2) we will have to make course corrections along the way. Just a hundred years ago, we didn't know but what a better hot-air balloon could take us to the moon. Now we make our own "moons" orbiting Earth and can consider a colony on Mars. This is a far cry from just a few hundred years ago, when we thought Earth was flat and people wouldn't venture far from home for fear of falling off the edge. Okay, some people may still believe Earth is flat, but you get the point. As you consider shooting for the moon, shoot for the stars instead and venture into business opportunities that have yet to be explored.

Early in my entrepreneur journey, I didn't have much of a vision. As an artist, I could turn pictures upside down and insight out, with more creativity than I could put on one canvas. But I didn't know how to transform my mindset into a vision. Thirty years ago, if someone told me I would be a business leader, successful entrepreneur, or creative thought leader, I'd have thought they were crazy. I loved art, but I never saw the benefit of encouraging the creative mind.

The "starving artist" paradigm has stifled people's passion to be creative and led them to accept mundane day-to-day jobs. In creative thinking, we can't allow ourselves to fall into the work "groove" that becomes a "rut" and eventually, a "grave." Set your mind free with possibility thinking and give something a try. Learn from your failures. Enjoy the adventure and refuse to give up. Learn from your mistakes and build upon your failures. Replace your creative can't-power with willpower, constantly seeking a better way.

Open the Imagination

Imagination is the amazing ability to see what isn't there. Many adults would ask, "If it isn't there, how can I see it?" Great question, because most people believe the saying: *Seeing is believing.* Actually, it can be the other way around.

Reed Hastings' great idea turned out to be a big failure. The foot mouse. He worked with designers and developed a hands-free mouse, operated entirely by a person's foot movement. Well ... as it turned out, people got leg cramps. And floors aren't always as clean as we would like. If you think your mouse gets nasty on a table, think about what might happen on the floor. But that failure did not stop Reed. His imagination continued to grow and eventually led to the creation of Netflix.

I know a designer who proposed a new product to a manufacturer's engineering department. Their response? "No, that's impossible." The designer had a clear picture of how the manufacturing process would work, but the engineers couldn't see it. Later, the designer showed Engineering a similar item that another manufacturer had produced. When they saw the sample, they said, "Oh, yes! We can make that." Sounds like "seeing is believing," doesn't it? But actually, the sample was merely the proof that was needed to stir Engineering's creativity enough to believe the designer. After that, Engineering could see what they hadn't seen before, and they produced the new product.

Points to Ponder

- Entrepreneurship parallels art: Like conducting a symphony, leading a business requires vision, creativity, and attention to detail.
- Ideas often begin with sketches: Successful ideas start with simple concepts that grow into something worthwhile.
- Perseverance leads to breakthroughs: Creativity with a never-quit passion will overcome fear and failure, making innovative successes possible.

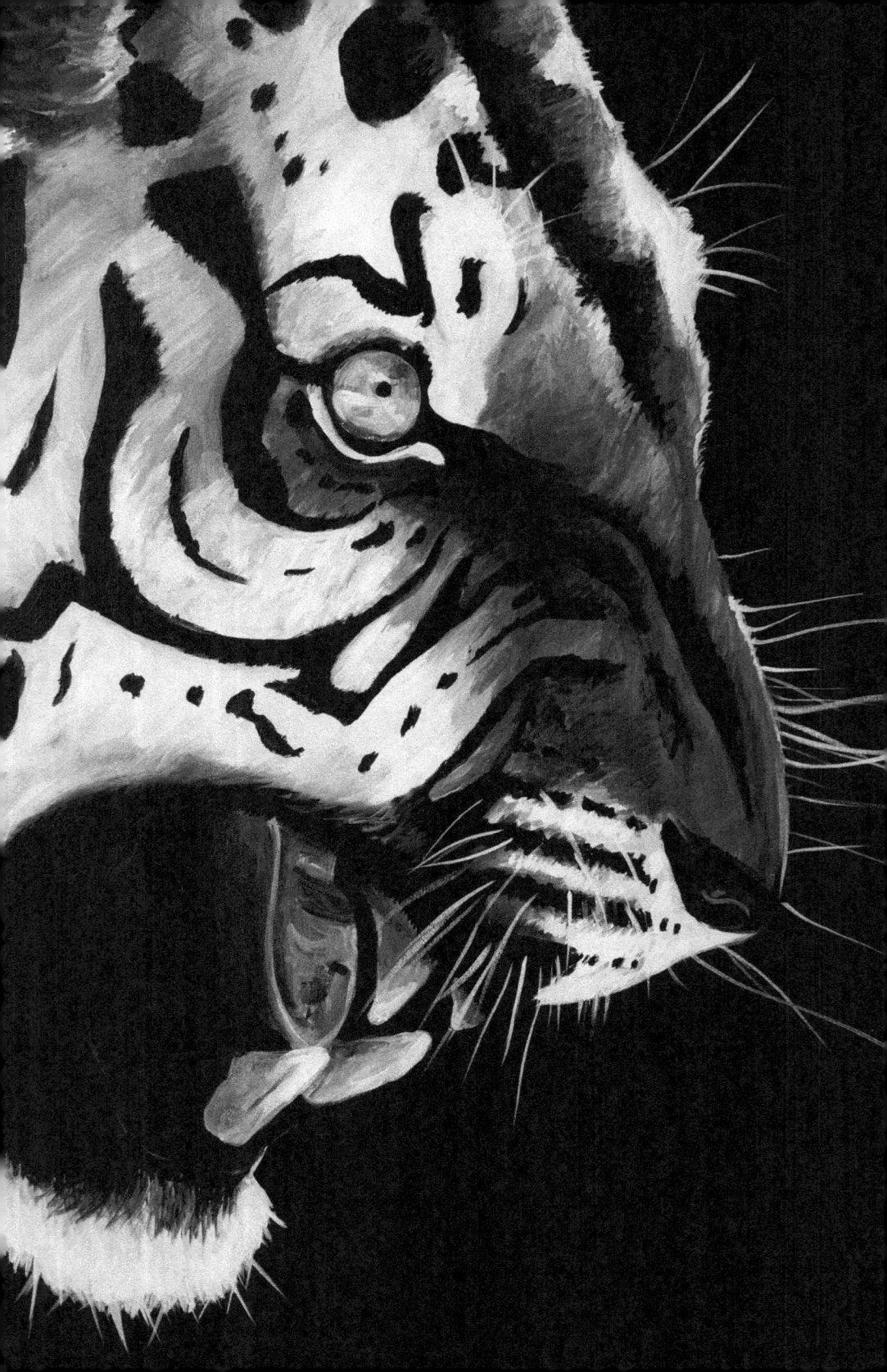

Adding Thought to the Canvas

I've known of entrepreneurs who sought to hire creative people because they thought the average employee wasn't capable of being creative. That wasn't true for me, and I don't think that's true for others. Unless we fight against it, everyone is naturally creative.

If children are fortunate enough to grow up in an environment that encourages creativity, they'll ask thousands of what-if questions. What's wrong with coloring outside the lines? Why can't a cow be purple? Who says it's not okay to draw people with matchstick legs and square heads? Tell such people that something can't be done, and they'll be looking for a way to do it. Thinking "outside the box" isn't a concern, because they don't know there is a box.

The unfortunate majority grow up having to follow rules. When a son asks why, Dad says, "Because I said so." Or a teacher says, "That is the assignment." Boundaries are drawn that dare not be crossed. Before long, with any idea slapped down as stupid, they accept what they are told and declare their misbelief: "I'm not creative."

We can't train a 4'5" college athlete to be 7'4" tall and dunk a basketball without his feet ever leaving the ground. The ability isn't there. But contrary to what some employers believe, creativity *can* be "trained," because we were all born with the ability to use our brains. We have different fingerprints, voiceprints, and thought patterns.

Not one person is exactly like anyone else on Earth. The first step toward creativity must teach that it's okay to be different. After that, the possibilities are endless.

Picasso is known for saying, "It took me four years to paint like Raphael, but a lifetime to paint like a child." Picasso may have learned from great artists, but his creative genius came from his willingness to be different.

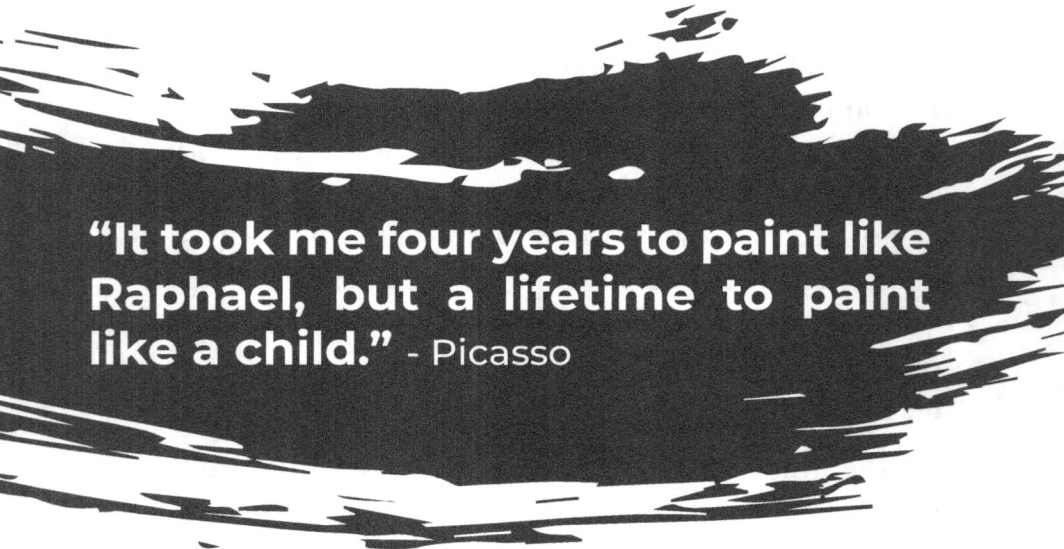

"It took me four years to paint like Raphael, but a lifetime to paint like a child." - Picasso

Kids are naturally creative. Their imaginations run wild with dreams of other worlds—stories of fairies, pirates, or a Jedi master saving the galaxy from the evil emperor. When we were young, we hadn't yet learned *impossibility* thinking. Today, we have movies and television to give us picture, sound, and action, leaving nothing to the imagination.

A Child's Imagination

Let's take a journey into our past. Try to remember your childhood fantasies. In those days, your toys could move and talk on their own. The characters from my toy-box, fought many wars. Battle after battle, Skeletor tried to conquer Castle Grayskull, but He-Man always came to the rescue.

The *Toy Story* movies are wonderful depictions of how our creative minds worked when we were young. In the third movie, Andy creates an elaborate train robbery that begins with Mr. Potato Head emerging with sacks of gold coins. Sheriff Woody catches Mr. Potato Head, but Mrs. Potato Head surprises Woody with ninja moves that knock Woody off the train. Of course, Bullseye and Jesse are there to catch him as he falls, or he might be forever broken. The Potato Heads mark their escape in Barbie's corvette, giving Woody a dilemma. As the story goes, every toy in Andy's room is pulled into an elaborate chase sequence.

Who wrote this story? How was it put together in movie frames? How was the music arranged? True artists strive to live in their world of childlike creativity. Just like Andy, you still have the same imaginative and artistic ability you had as a child. They're still there. They simply have been suppressed and need to be revived through opening up your mind to them again.

Opening Our Creative Minds

Those who didn't have the distractions of movies, TV entertainment, and video games relied on creativity to keep from being bored. Think back to when you were a kid and what you did when you weren't told what to do. On a vacation trip, did you visualize yourself doing things that you'd never done before? When you looked at the sky, did you see clouds, or were there furry animal shapes that grazed the blue field.

One day, my wife looked out the window and said to our youngest, "Do you see the unicorn in the clouds?"

"Yes!" she said excitedly, pointing. "It's right there. Look, I see a rabbit over there."

With a little encouragement, their imaginations ran wild. Notice that the human imagination is capable of seeing what isn't there, at least not literally. Not yet. But in the business world, we must open our creative minds to see what isn't yet there, or it never will be.

Better Than the Competition?

Many companies fail for lack of creativity. Their "success" depends on what they see others doing, which puts them at a competitive disadvantage. I'm all for learning from the artistic masters like Picasso did, but if your creativity can't produce something consumers can't get elsewhere, your ability to rise above the competition will be stunted.

An argument can be made that companies like Blockbuster lacked the creativity and vision to adapt to changes in the marketplace. First, Redbox and Netflix came onto the scene with kiosk services and mail-in DVDs. They quickly gained market share and grew in popularity because of the utilization of new technology.

When renting a movie, you knew you had to time it just right to get the new releases. Either you were in the store the day it released, or you planned out the times the rentals would be returned and scooped up the movie before others could rent it. Then technology evolved. Reserving your movie on an app without the hassle of not knowing if it was in stock or not was revolutionary. Having it delivered to your mailbox was even better. The signs were all around. It was just a matter of time before the ultimate end of Blockbuster.

Reed Hastings, co-founder and former CEO of Netflix, saw what was coming and had the ability to adapt along the way. DVDs and kiosks would soon be replaced with digital downloads. The only way Netflix could stay in the forefront was to produce their own content—not just any kind of content but top-of-the-line movie caliber content to compete with other players like Disney, with vast library of original content to share. Redbox was soon dead, and other leaders like Apple, Prime, and Disney were having to play catch-up. Each followed Netflix's lead and created their own platforms to share their unique content. Reed's ability to foresee what was coming was truly a work of visionary art.

Large companies often suffer from being stuck in how things were successfully done yesterday. They are quickly left behind for younger, creative ventures. It is only through enhancing our creative imaginations and the learning to adapt that our companies can gain the edge in the competitive world.

Sadly, our imaginations are easily hindered by parents, teachers, and coworkers, who continually remind us of what we can't do or shouldn't do. We're led to think our acceptance depends on joining the crowd and being like everybody else. Perhaps you were told to speak only when spoken to. In the classroom, you were to sit quietly in your seat and listen to the teacher. Don't ask a what-if question that deviates from the lesson, or you'll have trouble with the teacher. By the time we graduate college, we've learned so much about how everything has to be done that we've forgotten the joy of doing something that's not been done before. Our creative minds become suppressed through too many rounds of rejection.

Rejection-Proof

Be encouraged, because the artist in you hasn't died, but it might be asleep. Your creativity just needs some stimulation.

In his day, Monet's work wasn't acceptable. Why? Because he didn't paint like the masters. Pablo Picasso had the same problem. But subsequent history decided otherwise. What does that tell us? Try something new, and it may be rejected. When the telephone was invented, farmers saw no need. The first typewriters were more trouble than they were worth. Computers had value for very large companies, but nobody saw a need for one at home, let alone having one to carry wherever you went. Creative success comes only with refusal to give up with the first rejection.

When have you thought about turning off the country road, speeding across the gulley, and breaking through the barbed-wire fence to startle the grazing cows? Children might think of that, but adults know better. Instead, we're so focused on our destination, we can't enjoy the drive. Possibility thinking can be fun. We don't have to actually do what we're thinking. But give me a hundred of those ideas, and I might find at least one that would lead to something worthwhile.

The idea of painting like a child is not about immaturity or naivety, but rather about embracing the raw creativity and curiosity that children naturally possess. Their approach to the world is a sense of wonder and exploration, but adults restrain creativity. Picasso admired a child's perspective and wanted to capture it in his work by simplifying forms and focusing on the subject's essence, just like a child's drawing.

He believed every child is an artist, but the challenge lies in retaining that artistic spirit as one grows older. This highlights the importance of maintaining creativity and spontaneity in the face of the social pressures around us. By striving to paint like a child, Picasso aimed to preserve the raw, expressive power of art that comes from seeing the world with fresh eyes and expressing it without restraint.

Making changes can be difficult. Challenging, taking time. It won't happen overnight. But it can happen.

Just be ready for the challenge, because innovative thought can be met with detractors. You can't let unbelievers slow down your progress and growth. Remember, the most innovative entrepreneurs were rejected along the way, but they stayed true to their vision. Leaders embrace the true art of thinking outside the box, which has revolutionized our world.

Outside the Box

Your creative streak surfaces when you see your surroundings in a non-habitual way. Instead of the usual walk in the park, go where you don't normally go. What are the trees doing? What if they decided to do something else, having a mind of their own? Are the clouds watching you? What are they thinking? If they could talk, what would they say? The more you strive to be creative, the more creative you will be. And the more likely that your artistic creative genius will make you a better entrepreneur.

In today's world, most people know the names Elon Musk, Jeff Bezos, and Bill Gates. They've made a lasting impact on the world around them. One thing that makes them even more powerful is their ability to see things outside the box.

Bezos's determination was most evident in his approach to innovation and risk-taking. He encouraged a culture of experimentation at Amazon, understanding that failure was an integral part of the innovation process. This mindset led to the development of several groundbreaking services. One service in particular, Amazon Web Services, would become one of the keys to their success.

AWS became the major profit driver for Amazon. In 2021, accounting for 13 percent of Amazon's total revenue and contributing some 74 percent of its operating profit. By 2024, AWS achieved an annual revenue run rate of $100 billion, with a significant increase in operating income.

Amazon's use of data was immense, and they were able to see the opportunity to turn a major expense into a profit driver, which could have been easily overlooked. Someone had to look outside of the box.

What are some business areas you can rethink, which might turn expenses into a profit center?

Points to Ponder

- Creative thinking can be trained: You can't train people to be taller, but if you dare to be different, your childlike creativity can be nurtured back into good health.
- Innovation requires a fresh perspective: Successful companies like Netflix thrived from creative thinking and adapting to changes while Blockbuster failed to innovate.
- Rejection is part of the creative journey: Great artists like Picasso faced rejection but succeeded because he insisted on exploring new possibilities.

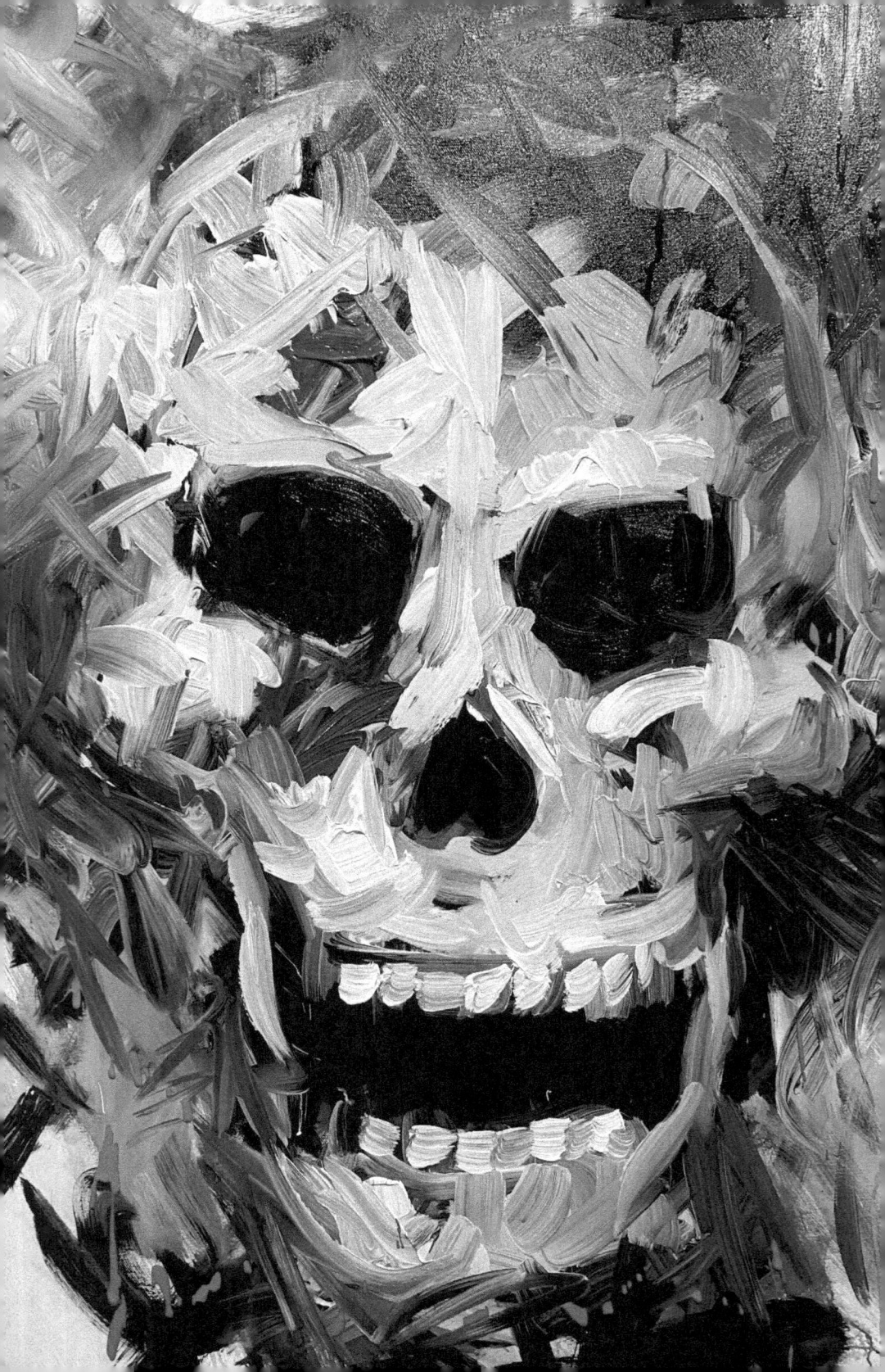

The
Inner
Critic

Our self-perception is the lens through which we view our potential. Those who tell themselves, *I can't*, create a self-fulfilling prophecy of failure, despite having the ability to succeed if they had believed they could. On the other hand, those who say, *I can do this*, may set themselves up for disappointment if what they think they can do is impossible. The crucial question is: How might our self-image be limiting our growth and keeping us from becoming our best? By challenging our inner critic and reframing our self-talk, we can see our potential and soar beyond what we had thought was impossible.

The art of an entrepreneur is refusing to accept the opinions of naysayers about impossibilities. An artist breaks through and turns impossibilities into possibilities. Far too often, we limit ourselves because of other people's thoughts and opinions when they truly do not matter. We can become who others think we are, putting on an act that leaves us far short of who we could become. Thes contrary opinions hold us back and enhance the idea of imposter syndrome in our lives.

Yoda of *Star Wars* fame said to Luke Skywalker, "Do. Or do not. There is no try." Without the doing, the thinking has no value, but without the believing, thinking you can, there is no proving of what is possible.

Impostor syndrome is a psychological term for those who see themselves as frauds, fearing exposure, doubting their skills and accomplishments, not believing they deserve their celebrity. The basketball player won the game at the buzzer, but it was a lucky shot, the ball bouncing off the backboard when he was aiming for the basket. Wayne Gretsky famously said, "You miss 100 percent of the shots you don't take." So the crucial action is to take the shot. Otherwise, you may miss an amazing opportunity in your life.

No matter how good we are, someone has a higher IQ, can move faster, or has more strength. In our desire to be our best, we can set ourselves up to never being good enough. At some point, we must recognize and accept who we are, with strengths and weaknesses, before we can visualize where we can go.

By tapping into the artist inside all of us, we can begin to become who we are meant to be—the pure unaltered creative child who dreams of taking the final shot. Counting ... 3 ... 2 ... 1. He shoots and scores the winning goal at the NBA championship. Day after day, kids shoot hoops on the playground back yard, fantasizing such a great success. Some days, they make the shot. On other days, they miss. But they never stop shooting, because that's the only path toward the feeling of victory. Then, so often as we grow older, our mind shifts into fear that we'll miss, and we don't have a chance at the winning shot.

Five kinds of imposters are worthy of highlight: The Perfectionist, The Expert, The Genius, The Lone Ranger, and The Super Hero.

The Perfectionist

For this kind of imposter, everything needs to be exactly right. Therefore, you strive for excellence in all you do. Others may look at you as the best of the best, but that's not the way you see yourself. In high school, a perfect test score left you in fear that you might not do as well next time. You might make a mistake, which is a fear that can be paralyzing.

You pay close attention to small details, which results in high-quality work that you often must outdo yourself. Your intense work ethic and desire for continuous improvement may earn the "workaholic" label, for which you can be proud since you have accomplished so much.

But the fear of failure encourages you to procrastinate or avoid tasks or situations where you might not excel. You may spend excessive time on minor details, striving for more than is possible. With unrealistic expectations, you and those who work with you can never be good enough, which puts a strain on relationships.

Striving for excellence is wonderful, but perfection is worse than an impossible dream. It's a nightmare.

As an artist, I try to reject perfectionism. My humanness allows my artwork to display a uniqueness you won't see elsewhere. The same can be said for my role as a CEO or business leader. I learn through my mistakes. My experiences are the artwork of the entrepreneurial journey.

The Expert

You may not be a perfectionist, but it's easy to feel a need to know everything so you can't be a failure. Of course, you're an imposter because you can't know it all. Since you must always appear to know, you hold strongly to your beliefs and reject opposing points of view. You would argue with a fence post. Okay, maybe you wouldn't. But you would if it could talk back and you could prove that you were right. Since you know there's more to learn, you boast of being an expert while feeling you're not.

It's easy to pose as an expert because it gives you authority and credibility. Your ideas and recommendations, perhaps no better than others, may be taken more seriously. Accolades and awards can boost your confidence and provide valuable opportunities.

With success comes accountability, insecurity, and the fear that you can't maintain the level of knowledge and expertise that others expect. Then your reluctance to accept perspectives other than your own can hinder creativity and innovation. If you are convinced that you already know, that your way is the only right way, then your personal and professional growth may be stunted.

Give credit where credit is due, seeking to learn from others because you don't know it all. You can share what you know because they don't know it all, either.

A true example of this lies in one of history's best basketball players. Kobe Bryant's work ethic is legendary. His workouts started as early as 4:30 a.m., while everyone else was sleeping. His commitment to mastering the fundamentals of basketball is a testament to how hard work can pay off. This dedication is often mentioned as a major reason for his success, which is confirmed by the stories shared by those who saw his routine.

Strength and conditioning coach Alan Stein attended Kobe's skills academy. He thought he left in time to view the start of Kobe's early-morning workouts, but no.

Kobe was already in a full sweat, having started his training long before Stein was told to arrive. Kobe's routine involved not just practicing advanced techniques but also a rigorous focus on the basics, such as footwork and fundamental offensive moves—for extended periods.

Stein was amazed and had to ask why he focused so much on the basics.

"Why do you think I'm the best player in the world?" Kobe said. "Because I never ever get bored with the basics." This highlights his belief that mastering the fundamentals was crucial to his success. His approach was about deliberate practice, where he meticulously worked on specific skills to perfect and keep them sharp, not just log so many hours of practice. He relentlessly pursued the elusive idea of perfection.

The Genius

Others might see you as brilliant as the likes of Kobe, but you know you're not. Whether it's being an expert or a genius, you may feel like a fraud. Because you know you're not naturally intelligent and creative, you have studied or worked hard for years to get where you are. You put the time in, working on the basics over and over. Attempt after attempt often failed. But you kept working until finally … success! Suddenly, you're seen as a genius because what you did actually worked.

People don't know how many times you've failed or all the work you put into the venture, but you know. At the same time, you feel lucky. You understand that no one else was able to do it, so you take ownership of the success.

Maintaining the genius façade can make you appear intimidating and unapproachable, but you don't want to be. Sometimes, this leads to missing valuable connections and friendships along the way. People assume you already know, so you miss learning what could help you the most.

Strive to improve rather than relying on a fabricated image of genius.

The Lone Ranger

You know what you do. You do it so well, and training someone would take too long, so you'd rather do it yourself. The more you do yourself, the more you learn. You have full control and deserve all the credit for your accomplishments. Problem is, there's more to do than you can possibly do.

By working alone, you limit your own creativity. Our brilliant thoughts are often sparked by someone else's idea. By doing the work yourself, your innovation suffers because you can't see how others could do the job better. Entrepreneurs may seek others to do the work they don't have time to do. A better choice is to recognize others who will do the job better if we give them the chance.

At times, I felt like the Lone Ranger, embracing the misbelief that if you want something done right, you do it yourself. Yes, I was known to say this out loud, and it did cause problems within our organization.

A Lone Ranger leadership mindset limits the growth of a company, because one person cannot possibly do everything that needs to be done. You become a bottleneck that hinders performance and growth, both in service to customers and in development of employee skills.

The only way to grow an organization is through empowering a team to grow beyond yourself. This means allowing them to fail in the ways you did along the way. Even the Lone Ranger had Tonto working alongside him, at times becoming his life-saving hero.

The Super Hero

In this imposter syndrome, you must be the hardest worker in the organization, the best in the family, and able to clear tall buildings in a single leap. You're here to save the day. Otherwise, you're a fraud. You live in fear that in the next situation, you won't measure up to people's expectations.

In high-pressure situations where immediate action is required, you may hesitate, second-guessing your actions. Self-doubt can impair your creativity and decision-making ability. You will find it more rewarding to make others into superheroes, not yourself. And that will make you a superhero from a different perspective.

Points to Ponder

- Empowering others is crucial: Personal and organizational growth will suffer when leaders have a Lone Ranger I-must-do-it-myself mindset.
- Fundaments are fundamentally important: mastery in any field of expertise requires dedication to the basics and continual refinement.
- Mistakes can make us better: Embracing mistakes is a vital part of learning and growth.

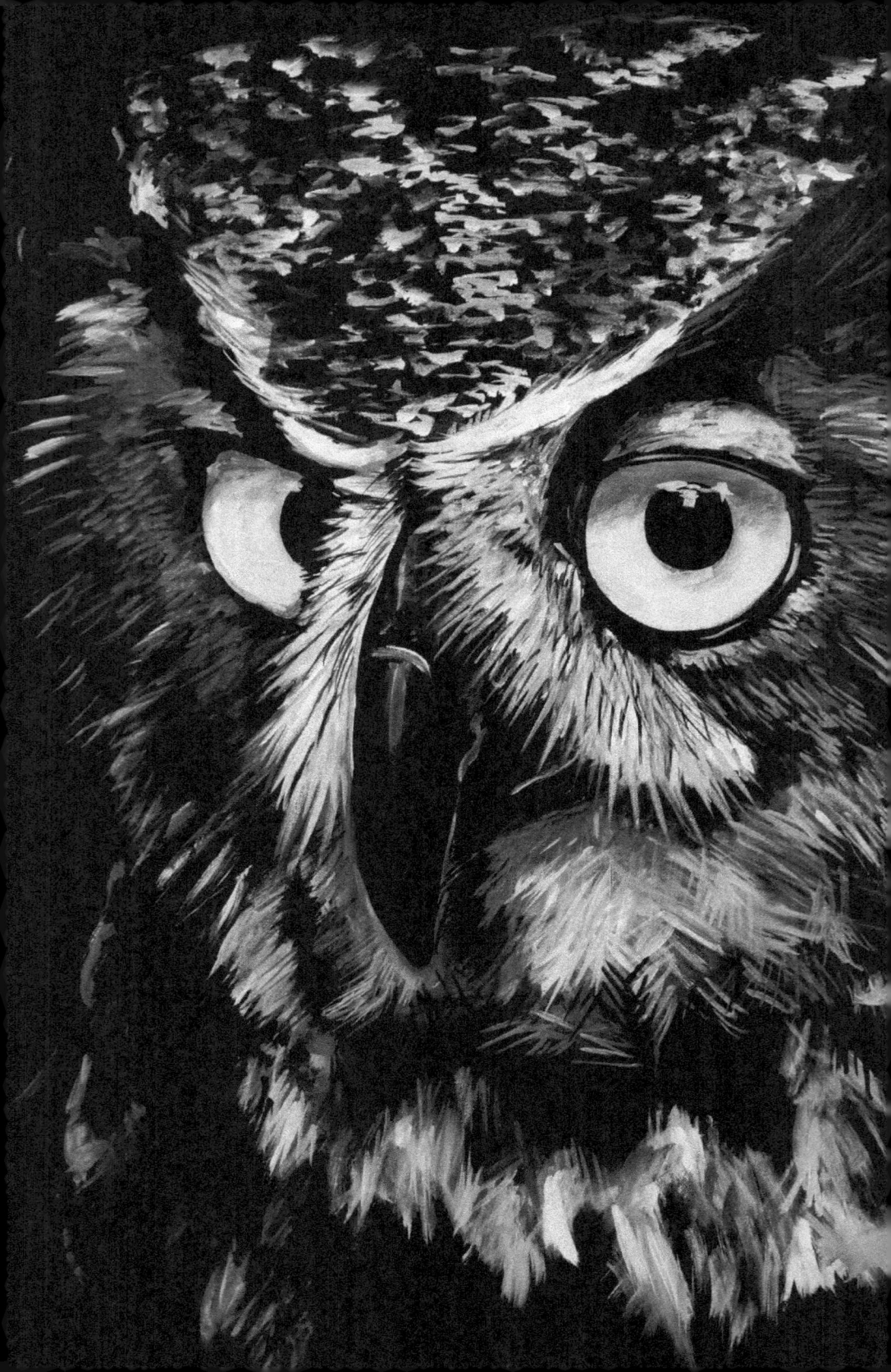

Depth of Vision

Without perspective, vision has no depth. With one eye, we see a picture like a photo, which has the *illusion* of depth. On a flat canvas, the wide city street in the foreground narrows to a single point on the horizon, giving the viewer a perception of depth even though every brush stroke is the same distance from the viewer's eye. With imagination, viewers can see themselves hurry down the sidewalk to work in the tall building that somehow seems more majestic when they are actually at the street corner, waiting for the light to change.

On the canvas, the tall buildings get progressively smaller as the street narrows, but that's not what people see on their walks to the office. With their own two eyes, they see the ten-story building on their block as the same height as the ten-story building four blocks away. With one eye, we have vision, but with two eyes, we have perspective.

Perspective beyond Vision

Vision is largely subjective, based on our limited point of view. What we learned growing up at home, our indoctrination in schools and churches, and the bias of modern-day media gives us a rather flat, limited picture of our world. From the window of your penthouse office, you can see much more than employees working on the first floor. You see people on the street shading their eyes and know the sun is bright. But can you see the rapidly developing low pressure that will bring a cold rain in the afternoon with the threat of hail? To know that, you must trust another perspective.

On the flip side, if you stay inside the penthouse office, you may never understand what is happening on the first floor or warehouse. Sometimes, to truly understand, you have to get your hands dirty and get back to the basics.

This is why TV shows like *Undercover Boss* were so powerful. Very successful CEOs disguise as new hires in the business. Show after show, CEO after CEO goes undercover, working in entry levels of the business, not knowing what they will discover within their own organization. Soon, these executives learned what was going on in the trenches, where the work was being done daily. Every CEO dealt with a different situation, but each had their eyes completely opened to what they couldn't see before. They walked away with greater empathy for their employees and a deeper understanding of the true culture of the company. The value of stepping out of the office and experiencing work from different business perspectives was priceless.

In business, vision is good, but it's one-dimensional. Perspective is much better because it's multi-dimensional, seeing from different directions and distances.

On-Stage Artist

As an on-stage artist with canvas and brush, I see shapes, colors, and textures much different from the audience seated far away. They see the development of the whole picture while I'm focused on a particular brush stroke. Because I am so close, I don't have the perfect perspective on how the painting should really look. Sometimes I have to step back to see what I can't see up-close. This is the proverbial problem of not seeing the forest because of all the trees. Up close, I can't even see the tree because what's important is one branch and the colors of its leaves in the sunlight.

On a mission trip to El Salvador, I was scheduled to speak and paint. Many foreign cultures don't have the American discipline for maintaining a dependable schedule. I arrived early and found out I was late. No time to mentally prepare. No chance to let the creativity build. With my nerves on edge, I walked on stage, only to learn that I had only five minutes to paint something that would be meaningful to the audience and would complement what I was to speak about.

With help from an extra flow of adrenalin, it was looking good. The painting was taking shape exactly as I intended. Then, I added some black to enhance the image. *Great*, I thought. Then I stepped back. *Oh, crap! I screwed it up!* It was BAD. What was I going to do? You can't just erase black paint. It needs to dry, and I had no time because I was about to speak. My mind raced through several scenarios, each one quickly dismissed.

How am I going to fix this? It's impossible. Then came an epiphany. What happened was perfect for what I was about to share: the importance of perspective.

I went on to speak about how we make mistakes in life. We fail. We struggle. Sometimes we think we're out of time. It's over. Guess what? The journey is not finished, and you are still in the midst of your destiny. Failure is not an ending but the beginning. Then, in the midst of the speech, I paused, went back to the painting, and fixed the mistake. I turned a failure into a masterpiece because I found a new perspective.

Your business looks a certain way from your perspective, but how will you handle the perspective of others? Does it matter? Yes, a little, because bad press can ground an airline, so it matters. No entrepreneur can be successful making decisions from a single perspective.

Buried in the day-to-day routine, you may not see the bright sun from where you sit. For your business to reach its full potential, you might need to get out more. See your world from other perspectives. Step back from your closeup vision to get a clear perspective of how your business can reach its full potential.

Calling the Plays

In professional football, each position sees the field differently. The running back knows what to do before the quarterback calls the play, but what do they see? The quarterback calls for the ball to be snapped, and everything changes. Now, the running back sees the backs of 300-lb linemen who are supposed to open space for him to run. The play tells him where he's supposed to go, but with perspective, he sees a better way and cuts at a different angle and direction. Suddenly, he breaks through, races down the field and reaches the end zone. In a matter of seconds, he becomes the hero by scoring the touchdown in violation of the "called" play.

Most often, it doesn't happen that way. The running back runs to where the gap is supposed to be and is tackled immediately. From the comfort of our armchair at home, we clearly see where he should have run. Because we have the perspective he didn't have, we yell at the screen, as if he should have seen the opening. All he had to do was reverse his direction, and the first down was assured. Now, our team must punt, and we blame the offensive coordinator for sending in a bad play. Who had the perspective? We did, but it does us no good, because we're not out there on the field.

As a business leader, we can always find someone to blame. We need a new quarterback, a new head coach, or someone else to call the plays. Maybe so, but many times, placing the blame can miss the real problem. Protect the quarterback so he has time to see the field before he's sacked. Send the running back into the flat where he can catch the ball and have room to run. As the head coach, you have great players. They just need help with perspective.

Failure's Not Final

Football and business are much like rollercoasters, with breathtaking ups and downs, twists and turns, and unexpected jerks that make you wonder why you chose to watch or ride. But here we are, like it or not. The worst we can do is let failure ruin our perspective to the point that we don't like the ride. We want to quit. Don't even think about it. Let your experiences, both good and bad, give you a better perspective.

Yoda of *Star Wars* fame said, "The greatest teacher, failure is."

In our early years of business, my partner and I didn't like the reality we were facing. Daniel McCarthy, our first employee had grown beyond his role and had become problematic within our company. We hired him at age nineteen and trained and nurtured for years, but he wasn't the team player we had hoped for. I guided him through every situation, even to a point where he was better pitching to customers than we were. But as much as I wanted him to be part of our success, I had to admit the truth. He was following his own path, and it wasn't going to work.

I felt like I was the one who had failed, not my employee and friend. Hands down, the hardest thing I'd had to do was letting him go. I struggled because this was the person I had invested everything into. What did I do wrong? Was it my fault? Thought after thought of failure haunted me.

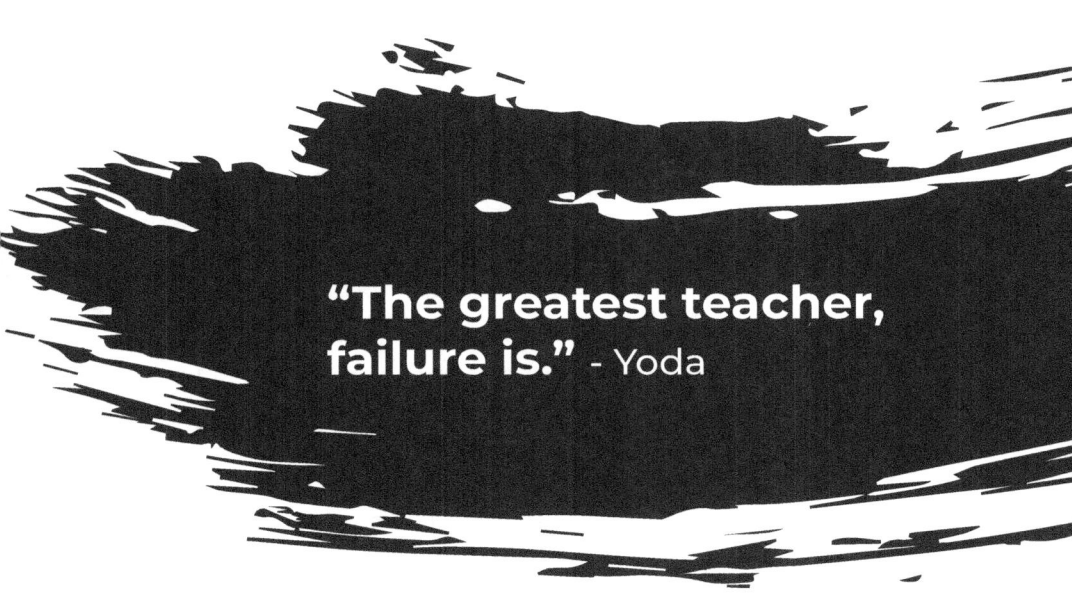

"The greatest teacher, failure is." - Yoda

What followed were two of the most difficult years I have ever been through as a business leader. Our work culture was dark and difficult as we had to work through situations and battle problems even though he was gone.

I had to make adjustments that I never anticipated. One-by-one, I picked up the pieces and learned to lead the business better. Now, I no longer see that first hire as a failure. I'm thankful to have had that experience early-on, because I learned so many important lessons that have helped our company thrive. It also allowed me to view situations from a different perspective and see areas of the business that needed vast improvement.

If the first hire and I hadn't parted ways, neither of us would be where we are today. He too became an entrepreneur, founding several eight-figure businesses, becoming more successful than I could have imagined, but we'll dive into that later.

The truth is, if we hadn't parted ways, neither of us would be where we are today. Sometimes holding on to things in the past benefits no one. Embrace failure, learning to change, and the future become a new world of opportunity.

Failure is not final. If it were, we would not have people like Steve Jobs, companies like GoPro and FedEx, and places like Disney World. With his early ventures, Walt Disney was fired from a newspaper job for "lacking imagination" and faced bankruptcy. However, his imagination would lead a world in creativity and innovation.

As a leader, you must find the answer to difficult situations. With creativity and imagination, step back and see what's missing. Learn from each failure. Dust yourself off and try again. Then, with a new perspective, what looked so bad before can reveal the steps needed to reach a higher level of success.

Points to Ponder

- Check out the mail room: Leaders gain by stepping out of their high-level roles to gain insights from the employees who are working to meet customer needs.
- Turn mistakes into opportunities: Like the artist's painting, errors can be reframed into positive outcomes when they are viewed from a different perspective.
- Know when rules need to be broken: Like the running back on the football field, a better perspective can break through the defense and score with a play that was never called.

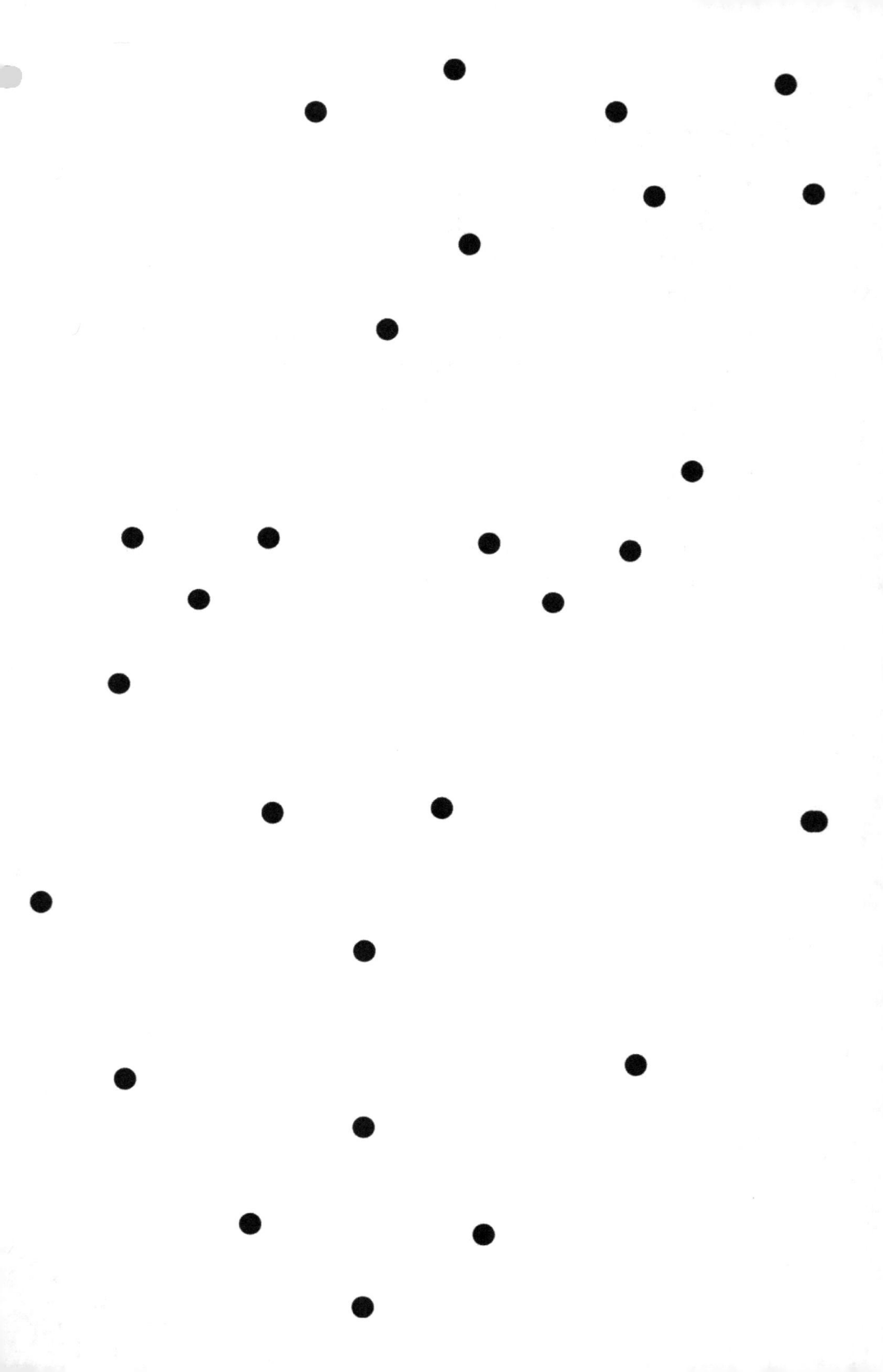

Connecting the Dots

Having a clarity of vision and perspective are part of the Art of Entrepreneurs, but many can do something others cannot. Connect the dots.

As a kid, I loved connecting black dots scattered on a white page to discover a hidden picture. This required counting ability and no artistic skill because each of the dots was numbered. Simply draw a line from dot 1 to 2, 3, and 4, continuing until the picture takes form. If the dots hadn't been numbered, they would be like stars at night. Without numbers, I had to recognize the patterns that formed different constellations. First, I found the Big Dipper, then the Little Dipper and the North Star. By learning to connect the unnumbered stars, I could locate the distinctive W or M pattern of Cassiopeia, the bright stars of Orion, and the keystone shape of Hercules.

Before I could create a picture, I had to visualize how to connect the dots. With practice, I learned to draw any number of pictures using a random scattering of dots.

In a similar way in business, we must see people where they are and see how they fit the overall picture of the enterprise. With creative vision, we can make better connections than what we might have previously thought impossible. So let's see if we can stimulate our creative minds.

Three Dots

Place three dots on a blank sheet of paper. What picture first comes to mind? A triangle. That's it. Ordinary people stop there, satisfied that they have the only correct solution.

Actually, the possibilities are endless. We just have to break the paradigm that the dots must mark where three straight lines connect. Then, with just a single line, not three, we can draw a circle, ellipse, parabola, square, trapezoid, sine wave … or come to think of it … just about anything, including a bowl full of spaghetti.

What we have here is what we have in business, unlimited possibilities of choices and actions that shape who you can be as an entrepreneur. People with vision accept where the unmovable dots are and visualize a workable picture. Sometimes they work and sometimes they don't, but the important part is seeing what *might* work so it can be tested.

Scattered Dots

Suppose we have a page with dots scattered at random. What do you see? Most people see a bunch of dots. Just like the night sky, they see a bunch of stars. Well … they *could* see them if they weren't looking up through the city's bright lights. Why don't average people see more? Because our brains have been trained to see dots as beginning and ending points for straight lines. Allow curves to pass through the dots, rather than starting or stopping there, and we have unlimited possibilities.

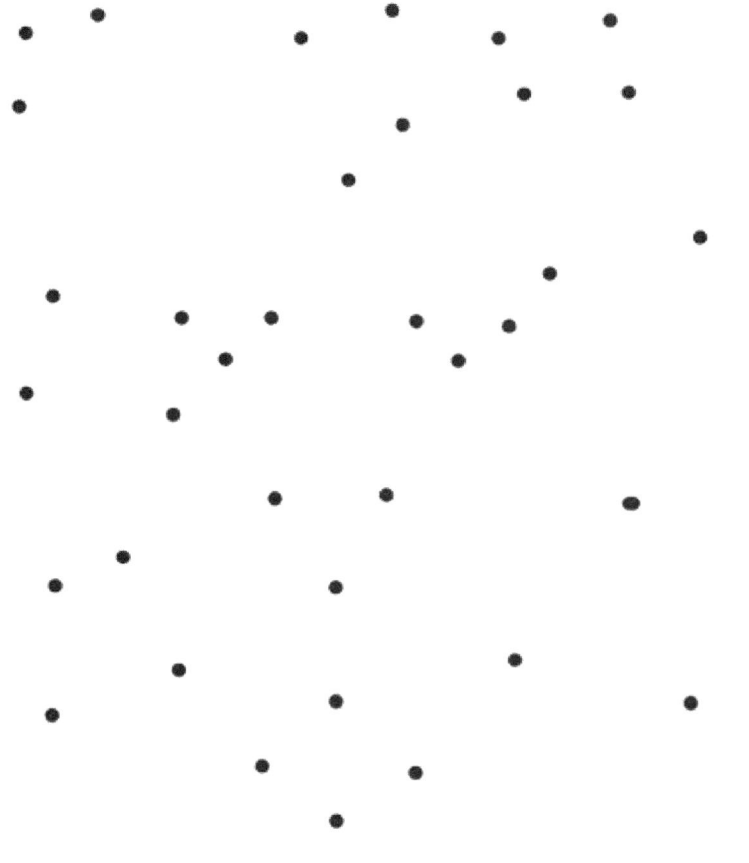

In the entrepreneur's journey, we have lots of dots with no clear path or direction. In the sample above, what do you see. A white sheet of paper after facing a shotgun blast. No, seriously. Let your mind see curves instead of straight lines, passing *across* the dots instead of ending there. Do you see where a mouth or nose might be? Now that you've seen the lines, the picture has potential. How did we get there? Ideas come from seeing what isn't there … but it could be.

Not all ideas are good ideas, but I can tell you that we can easily dismiss a good idea as bad only because we think more about what the picture might become. What do we have so far? A dog? A cat? Or just some modern art that isn't supposed to make sense? If a cat, 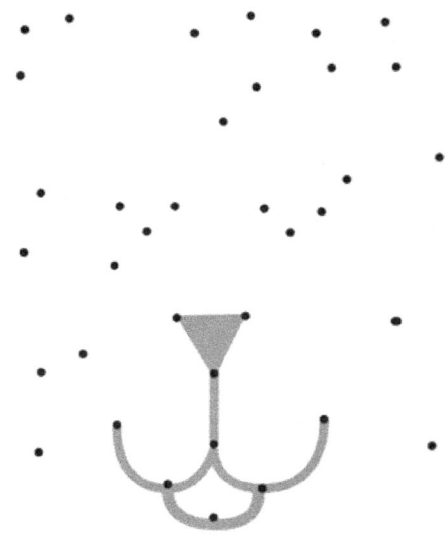 where would we put the eyes, certainly not toward the side where the ears would be. Ah, yes. I see two sets of three dots that might be about where the eyes would be. What shape are the eyes? Triangular? Round? Oval? Even square? With three dots, you can form whatever shape you might like. Let the creative part of your mind go as you stare at the dots, something like staring at the Milky Way at night. Don't rush to finish. Let your concept develop until you reach that *aha!* moment.

The first time I did this exercise, I moved too quickly and created a stick figure similar to a knight holding an ax. The second time, I saw what might be an arm. With a closer look, I saw two heads. Soon, I had drawn two people in an embrace. When I finished the picture and looked at the whole, I saw an abstract, smiling face—two pictures in one. This was an image I couldn't plan, but the exercise led me into a deeper creative experience. The process of unlocking your creativity will flourish as you focus on possibilities.

Your vision can never be exactly the same as anybody else's. In fact, from one day to the next, you're likely to see something different all by yourself. So never stop looking for something new. This is the beauty of the art behind the entrepreneurial journey. We all have different paths to get to similar destinations.

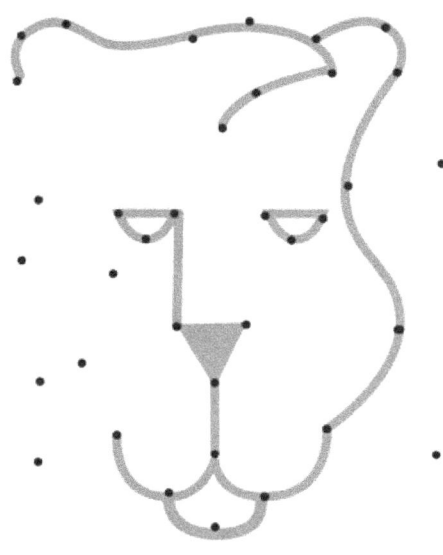

They'll never be the same, which suggests that you should never copy others, thinking their success guarantees your success. Learn from them, but copying seldom works like you might think it should.

Melanie Perkins, co-founder of Canva, is a great example of an entrepreneur who spotted a need, connected the dots, and turned an idea into something extraordinary. While she was studying at the University of Western Australia, she noticed her classmates struggling with the clunky, complicated design software used in their projects. That's when it hit her—there was a real gap in the market for a design tool that was simple and accessible to everyone.

Perkins didn't waste any time. She launched Fusion Books, a platform that made it easy for students and schools to create their own yearbooks. It was a hit, but she knew she could take this idea further. She had a bigger vision—a comprehensive design platform that would simplify graphic design for everyone, not just students.

Even though she was rejected continuously by investors along the way, when Canva officially launched in 2013, it quickly attracted over 100,000 users and saw 1.8 million designs created by the end of its second year. Fast forward to today, and Canva is a global phenomenon with millions of users and a valuation in the billions.

Melanie Perkins' story is a testament to the power of recognizing a need, seeing the potential in a simple idea, and turning that vision into a reality with relentless determination. She connected the dots and created a tool that changed the way the world designs, even when the rest of the world hadn't realized it was needed.

Start with something. Any dot anywhere. Don't let fear keep you from trying. Failure is just the beginning. See what works. You can't find out without failing a few times. Maybe lots of times. So test your ideas as early as possible. Spend a million dollars on an idea, and you'll be obligated to spend another million trying to make something work that never will. Just keep connecting dots and learn what will pull the picture together. Sometimes our dreams need adjustment, but no worries. With adjustments and redirection, you can fulfill your dream to the last dot.

The Essential Tool

Connecting the dots is not something that is always taught. Sometimes colleges and universities teach everything but what is most important after graduation. Students learn who, when, and why. They study what, where, and how. But if they haven't discovered the importance of continuous improvement and how to keep learning, they haven't learned enough. Entrepreneurs must keep bettering themselves because the world can change rapidly.

With ebooks and audio, digesting book content has never been easier or more affordable, both in dollars and time. What dots are you struggling to connect? You can be sure there's a book written about that. Hiring a coach can bridge the gap between dots. Joining a mastermind or peer group can keep you on the right path. But ultimately, it's up to you to keep going in the right direction and make adjustments along the way.

Revisit your vision. Where are the weaknesses? What are the strengths? We can let ourselves become so busy doing the work that we neglect the crucial points that keep us from our goals. Take a walk. Enjoy the silence at the park. Free your creative mind. Then write, draw, or diagram what isn't there, but remember, it could be. Commit to finding answers every day, and you will be amazed at your growth potential. Are you committed to your journey and the destination you set for yourself? If so, document it and find some accountability.

As with many people, accountability is vital for me to stay on pace. I easily distract myself with things to do, filling my day with both important and not-so-important tasks. Being busy doesn't mean I'm being productive.

I love fitness and my CrossFit gym because of the relationships and accountability I have built over the years. I have coaches who push me to get better. The same principle applies to nutrition. On my own, I can create a meal plan and see moderate results. But when I hired a coach, the results were huge. What made the big difference? Accountability!

The entrepreneur's journey should not be traveled alone. We need people walking with us ...

who see what we might have missed,

who care about our struggles and successes,

who will challenge us to stay on the right path,

who won't allow us to slack off, who will celebrate our successes,

who won't let is sit back and coast, who won't let our vision fade.

You want a coach who will take you to the Super Bowl, who will help you with your putter or driver so you can win the Master's. You get the idea. You want a coach who will bring out the best of what you can do. Connect the dots with those who will get you there.

Numbered Dots

Connect-the-dot books are a fun activity for children to practice counting, develop patience, and encourage imagination and creativity. They find patterns in the randomness so eventually, if all goes well, they learn to handle the dots without the numbers.

Workers who punch a timeclock and depend on supervisors to tell them what to do are comfortable with randomness as long as someone is there to number the dots. Entrepreneurs have a different mindset, enjoying the excitement of a discovery that is possible only when the dots aren't numbered.

How might the dots be connected? When we have the numbers already assigned, we have only one possibility. But without the numbers, any picture is possible. It all depends on what we choose to do with the dots. That's the art of the entrepreneur, to decide how the dots should be numbered—which ones are of primary importance and which ones provide necessary support before the picture can be complete.

Through unpredictable twists and turns, through peaks and valley, through what doesn't work as much as what does … we learn. We see enough of the picture to visualize success. As you keep connecting the dots, you must know the impossibility of seeing the whole picture from the beginning. Even the child looking at the numbered dots will struggle to visualize the picture before any lines are drawn to connect the dots. So don't lie to yourself at any point of seeming failure, saying, *I should have known*. That's an argument against reality. You can't know until it all comes together, one connection at a time.

When the journey is complete, the picture is clear. The dots represent defining steps in your life. Some are pivot points where you deviated from the original plan, either to survive or to create something even bigger and better. No matter what each dot may represent, they are crucial for your success. Don't fix them. Learn from them and let the picture and the creativity unfold.

The Road Ahead

Truth be told, if from the beginning you could have seen all the pitfalls, valleys, and obstacles, you might never have begun this venture. But here you are. You've come this far, paid such a high price to get here, and have learned so much. The future may not be easy, but you are better equipped to handle whatever lies ahead.

The road ahead is never clear, even if you had a map showing how to reach your destination. Why? Obstacles. A GPS might show a detour when you need to avoid a traffic jam, but neither it nor you can know about that until it happens. Nevertheless, with each challenge that can't foresee a future hazard, you succeed or fail at something new and become a better you.

Obstacle races are a great example. Each race presents new challenges, even if you've run before. I have run the Spartan, Tough Mudder, and Savage Race numerous times. Prior to the race, I'm given a map showing distances and obstacles along the winding trail—uphill, downhill, or through a creek bed. Each obstacle is represented as a dot on the map. In preparation, I visualize how I will pace the runs and handle each point. At the starting line, the emcee gets everybody energized. The music is blaring, and the energy is high. Runners are jumping, flexing, and running in place, preparing for that moment when they are on their marks. Then 5 ... 4 ... 3 ... 2 ... 1 ... and we're off. The fast runners try to separate themselves early. Sometimes too fast. Many lose their stamina and quickly fade.

After a mile and the first obstacle, my heart rate is

up. I climb over one seven-foot wall. Then another. And another. Each obstacle drains a little more from my energy storehouse, and I'm only getting started. Thirty more obstacles left, a daunting number that says I should quit. I fight with my mind and push on. Ten obstacles are now behind me, and I'm deep into the race. Fatigue starts to set in, but I refuse to give up. Then, something remarkable happens. A fresh boost of energy comes from somewhere. I don't know how or why, but it's there. After five more obstacles, the finish line is in view. I kick into a higher gear that I wasn't sure I had.

At the finish line, I'm totally exhausted. A great sense of accomplishment and satisfaction consumes me like a fire. I did it.

The Spartan Beast was by far the hardest race I have ever done. Every time I have asked, *Why am I doing this?* But I never failed to finish a race. Why? Because each one challenges me to do something great and to push myself out of my comfort zone.

Meeting the Challenge

Running a business seems to me much like running a grueling race, nowhere close to as easy as it looked at the start. The initial excitement is quickly lost in the face of obstacles that stretch us to the limit of our strength. But from somewhere, we summon more strength. True entrepreneurs can't quit. We must press on, overcoming each obstacle, passing dots like achievement markers and tackling each problem head-on. Looking back, we sense accomplishments from what our failures have taught us.

Maybe your obstacle is a sales call, a radical idea, or a business proposal. Whatever it is, the fear that held you back is now behind you. You have scaled that wall and can do it again. Now it is time for the next dot, the next challenge.

As you run toward the next goal, prepare yourself for both the expected and the unexpected. There will be challenges. Guaranteed. Find comfort and confidence in knowing you have the creative ability to achieve anything you set your mind to. You won't give up. You can't give up, even when the obstacles take you out of your comfort zone.

Preparation Is Key

You must put yourself through a fitness regimen. Anyone who would even think about running the Spartan Beast without first getting into shape would be insane. Oh, wait. I did that, didn't I? And I learned from that mistake. Lack of preparation makes the journey much more difficult. And sometimes impossible.

Start small and build up to the more difficult challenges. Starting small allows you to build strength and stamina to run a bigger race. Jumping into a race without preparation can leave you exhausted and defeated. You may have a Big Hairy Audacious Goal, but smaller milestones need to mark your journey. You don't need giant steps. Baby steps will get you there, often more effectively. So, take baby steps on your creative journey until bigger steps become comfortable.

Bill Gates and Microsoft's early BHAG of "a computer on every desk and in every home" is a perfect example. Given the state of technology and market penetration, this goal was certainly audacious at the time. But Gates approached this BHAG by taking incremental steps.

First, Microsoft developed software for the emerging personal-computer market, focusing on creating user-friendly operating systems and applications. Key partnerships with hardware manufacturers, such as IBM, ensured Microsoft's software would come bundled with new computers, gradually increasing market presence. This one step would be key to the eventual domination of the PC market. Lastly, Microsoft continually improved its software offerings, releasing new versions with enhanced features, which helped maintain its competitive edge and drive widespread adoption. Slowly adding new features gave the team time to creatively plan for each new improvement. It also gave them the perfect opportunity to give users the incentive to upgrade and pay for the new features.

The more steps you take, the more dots you can connect, leading to experience, and experience is the best teacher.

The Missing Dots

Before we leave this connect-the-dots concept, we should talk about the dots we need but aren't there. A blank page has no dots. What do we do now? Create them. What if some dots are in the way? Move them or delete them. As the entrepreneur, you set the rules about dots and what connects them. The lines can be straight, curved, or wavy.

Steve Jobs famously said, "You can't connect the dots looking forward. You can only connect them looking backward."

Understanding and predicting how current experiences will fit in the future can be hard. Only by looking back do they make sense. Ultimately, we must trust the process and continue to move forward regardless of what happens.

Steve Jobs probably never predicted his demise from Apple in 1985. At the time, his future seemed bleak, and the dots were unclear, but the journey was not over. He later described it as a pivotal moment that led to a period of creativity and innovation. It spawned companies like Pixar, which have been revolutionary. Pixar has created some of my favorite movies ever.

Look forward and connect the first dot to the next. Continue to move forward, adding more points to expand your picture. Think outside the normal three-dot triangle or the four-dot rectangle. Push yourself to see your future far beyond what you thought was possible.

Your creative genius is already inside you. Maybe the dots are invisible to you right now, so use your imagination. With fresh creative thinking, you can release power that will change your world. It won't happen overnight, but if you keep looking, your imagination will begin to connect the dots in ways you never thought was possible.

Points to Ponder

- Thrive on creating your own path: Unlike people who follow numbered instructions, entrepreneurs must define which dots are important and make unique connections without a predefined guide.
- Adapt to change: Successful entrepreneurs see connections, adapt their ideas, and refine their visions to meet marketing needs.
- Create new dots: Sometimes, opportunities for success don't yet exist. With continuous exploration, entrepreneurs use their imaginations to fill the gaps and connect new possibilities with the dots that already exist.

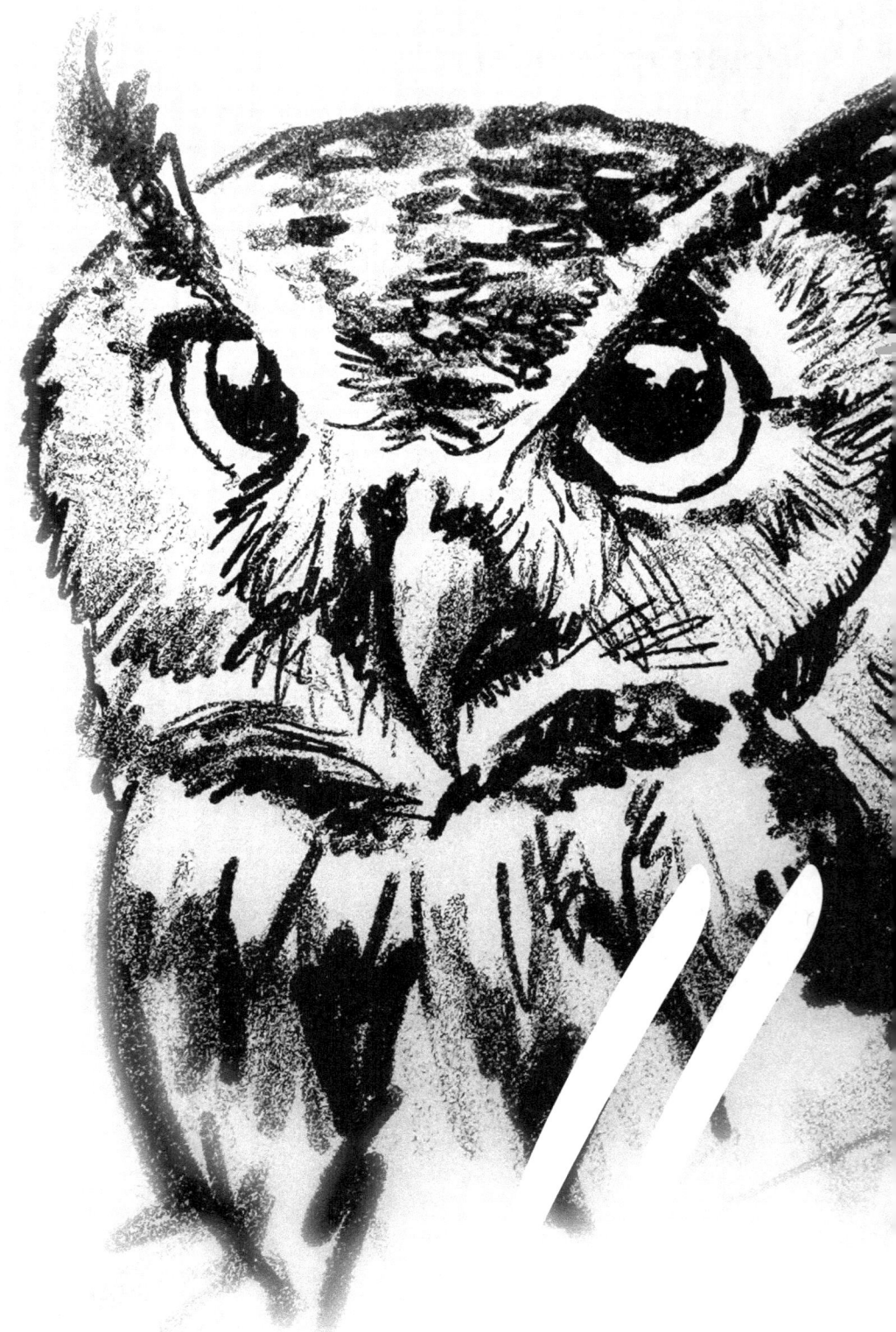

Sketching
the Blueprint

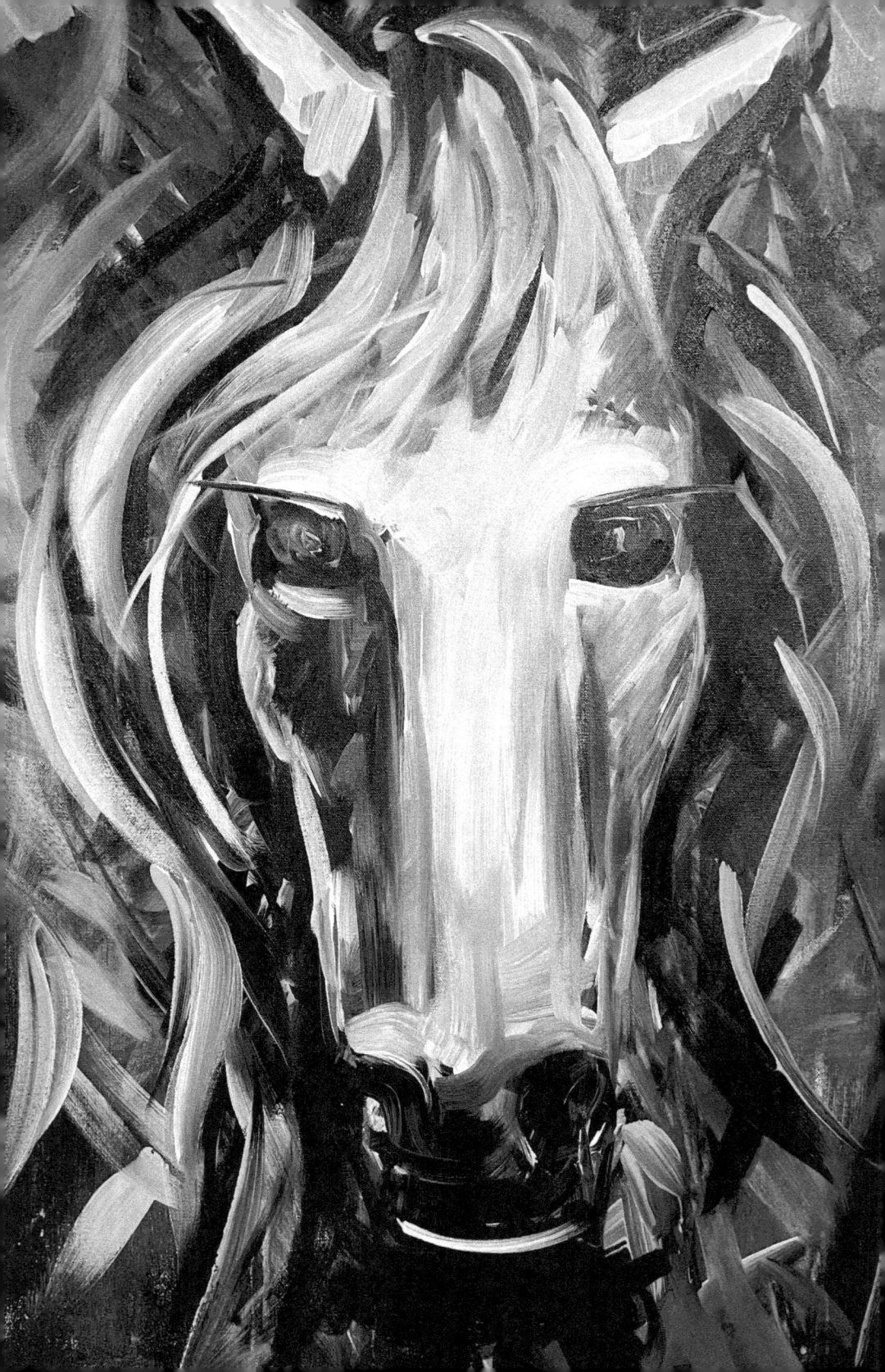

The
Faulty
Plan

We've all experienced that pivotal moment when, midway through executing our meticulously crafted plans, we admit that our blueprint is fundamentally flawed. This revelation isn't a mark of failure, but a rite of passage in the entrepreneurial journey. I've stood at this crossroads many times. Though initially disheartening, they challenge us to reassess, pivot, and transform our visions into something more robust and aligned with reality.

A Crazy Idea

Each spring when I was young, I looked forward to the father-son campout hosted by my church. I got to spend time with my dad, which was somewhat of a rarity because he seemed always to be working. Maybe it was my Indian blood that led me to appreciate sleeping in a tent among racoons, coyotes, and skunks. Far away from the city, I could see the stars at night and let the tree frogs serenade me until I fell asleep. I could hang out with friends and spend hours on the lakeshore, fishing. I was destined for a sunburn and this was the cost of being in nature.

One year, the group went to Inks Lake State Park near Austin, Texas. At this point, we were older and wanted bigger experiences. I was told we could drive around to a great swimming spot, where the high cliffs were perfect for daredevil cliff jumping. My dad had gone to tour an historic cave, so I jumped into the back of the pickup going the other way.

We had the greatest time, taking turns jumping off the cliffs about twenty-five feet above the water. After my first flying leap, my bravery was well-established. Repeatedly doing can-opener dives that shot a burst of water over ten feet into the air led to splitting open my shorts from seam to seam. It didn't matter, because I was having so much fun. After working up an appetite, I was ready to head back to camp. I looked for the pickup, but it was gone—now at the camp, on the other side of the lake.

From where I stood, the camp across the water seemed close. I could see the rock formation in the distance and thought, *We're all were good swimmers, right?* I said to the guys, "It's not that far. Swimming there would be a lot more fun." Most of them took the long walk back along the road, but a few liked my idea.

The first part was easy and fun, but then we faced a headwind that was pushing against us, cutting back our forward progress. What I thought was short swim turned about to be almost a mile, which soon told me that this would be much harder than hiking for ten. Near the cliffs, I hadn't noticed the wind and waves. Now out in the open, I faced a challenge I hadn't anticipated. To be safe, the other guys turned toward the shallow water near to the shore. I didn't go with them. Yes, I was tired, but I was committed, and I thought it wasn't that much farther. I *was* getting closer, and I'd be there before long. I just couldn't give up.

Swimming straight toward the camping spot took me farther and farther from the shore, but that was okay. The shortest distance between points A and B is a straight line, in this case across deep water. Then, out in the middle of the lake, there was no hope in turning back. I had to keep swimming straight ahead, pacing myself—at this point, not wanting to drown. After what seemed like two hours, I arrived at the rocky shoreline near the camp, totally exhausted. Slowly, I pulled myself out of the water and collapsed, thankful I hadn't died. Considering the difficulty of the swim, I certainly could have.

Could I have had a crazier idea? No. I think the only reason I made it to shore was my will to survive.

Tougher than It Looks

I've had other crazy ideas, but none so life-threatening. I'd like to think I am older and smarter now. I'm doing well with the "older" part, and I'd like to think I'm wiser. I've learned to be cautious when I think reaching a goal will be easy, both for business and pleasure. Ignorance isn't bliss. What I don't foresee can get me into bad trouble.

Sara Blakely's journey with Spanx is a story that mirrors the metaphor of a long swim across a lake. Starting with excitement and optimism, she was met with unexpected challenges that required perseverance to reach her goal.

Her idea for Spanx came when she noticed a gap in the market for comfortable, slimming undergarments. She saw the potential for a product that could revolutionize women's fashion, much like swimmers setting their sights on the distant shore, believing it's easily within reach.

But as she began her entrepreneurial journey, she faced wave after wave of obstacles. Potential manufacturers dismissed her idea, failing to see the value in her product. Getting her product into stores proved equally challenging, with buyers skeptical of her vision. For two years, she worked out of her home while selling fax machines to make ends meet.

Despite these setbacks, she tackled each obstacle with relentless persistence, personally demonstrating her product to store managers and refining her pitch until it resonated. Her persistence reminds me of the determination I needed to survive by reaching the shore.

Her focus and hard work paid off, but only because she refused to give up. Her big breakthrough came when she met a buyer from Neiman Marcus, leading to Spanx stocked in major department stores. Finally, she had reached the shore after a long and grueling swim.

The entrepreneur's journey will be filled with ups, downs, and sideswiping obstacles. That is what makes the journey a work of art. Seeing the goal is just the beginning. That Big Hairy Audacious Goal is achievable. But watch out. Getting there can be far more difficult than you imagine. There will be traps ahead, ones that could derail your journey if you are not focused and prepared for the worst you can imagine.

The Creative Journey

Before starting a journey, you do well to know where you are, where you're going, and how you're going to get there, which means you must "chart your course." You want to identify potential traps, problems, and opportunities. The more you can identify at the start, the more prepared you can be. Look closely. Our creative ability to see what isn't there allows us to see what is easily overlooked or what *might* develop later. Before my insane thought that I could swim across the lake, I could have seen the waves I'd be facing. Instead, I saw the calmer waters sheltered by the high cliff. This is what we call *short-sightedness*, a natural trait that is easily overcome with a creative mindset.

As a powerful leader, you must be a visionary, seeing both the problems and the opportunities ahead. Otherwise, you won't see the speed bumps coming your way.

Slow Down for Faster Speed

An old English proverb says, "Haste makes waste." In a hurry to get something done, we often act without thinking and wind up losing valuable time correcting our mistakes. On the other hand, fear of making mistakes can be paralyzing, proving that those who hesitate will suffer great loss. Hurry up? Slow down? What should we do?

Here's the good news: solutions come quickly to the creative mind, so nothing is lost by slowing down enough to consider what to do when the going gets tough. Rest assured, at some point the going *will* be tough. Facing such times in the past, did you panic, not knowing what to do? Or did you immediately consider your options, make the best choice, and work through the problem? The process may be difficult, but I promise, the more you slow down to think creatively, the more your genius will grow and the better equipped you will be to handle unexpected problems.

I'll never forget that swim across Inks Lake. Would I do it again? No, I've learned my lesson. I wouldn't fall into that trap again, not unless it was a life-or-death reason. With that experience, I'm more creative than I used to be. I'd slow down enough to think and know that the fastest path between two points isn't always a straight line.

The Impossibility Trap

One of my favorite artists was an expert in showing how two points can look like more than a straight line. M. C. Escher was a Dutch artist specializing in woodcuts, lithographs, and mezzotints, well-known among scientists and mathematicians for his treatment of symmetry, perspective, and geometry. In my high school geometry class, I was given a *tessellation* project, which required an arrangement of shapes closely fitted together in a repetitive geometric design, without gaps or overlap. My focus was art, so I was delighted to have an art project in a math class. I already loved Escher, so this was a dream come true.

Escher was a master of tessellation, with a wealth of source material to use for inspiration. I studied his *Reptiles* lithograph and drew wolves that metamorphosed to perfectly fit together in a repetitive geometric pattern. I was okay at math, and I loved geometry for its value in graphic design. We tend to excel at what we love, so yes, I aced the project.

I was mesmerized by Escher's ability to portray the impossible, like his continuous staircase and the waterfall that defied gravity. His mind-bending and illusionistic work helped me see how that what others thought was impossible was actually possible.

The trap is believing you can't, only because you've not tried. Or you failed on the first few tries and were too easily convinced that "you can't." So you've never created a beautiful pattern like Escher. Can you draw a stick figure? Earlier, we established proof that you can, especially as a child. Study Escher for a while, and you can imagine how to add color and shape in a repetitive design. As soon as you can imagine how, you've begun to escape the *I can't* syndrome. After that, it's just a matter of practicing your creativity.

Dealing with the This-Is-Too-Hard Trap

As a toddler, the first thing I had to learn was how to walk. After that, running became easy. Then I could run long distances. There may be limits to our physical abilities, but with good coaching and practice, we are almost always able to do much more than we imagined. We might even earn a place among Guinness World Records.

After learning to walk, I couldn't ride a bike. I was doing well to get on one. Did I just say *I couldn't*? Actually, I *was* capable, but to start, I used training wheels. I just didn't believe I could ride without them, not until after I saw my brother zipping up and down the street. First, I had to overcome my fear of falling. I saw my brother do it. If he could do it, so could I. That was all it took for me to dump the training wheels, pick up the bike, and go. Before long, with one foot pedaling after the other, I moved forward faster and faster. This was amazing. Now I just need to learn how to stop.

If at any point, we say to ourselves, *I can't* or *This is too hard*, we succumb to our weaknesses, not our strengths. What's the alternative? If you're looking, you can find a way. You're sure not going to find it by not looking, because can't see through the wall of impossibility.

The more time you spend learning and practicing, the better you will become. Get onto the bike, add the power of influence and the possibilities expand exponentially.

Creative Genius

Escher's art created illusions and imaginary worlds through angles, shapes, and lines. In his piece, *Relativity*, he challenges human intellect with staircases going in different directions and angles to impossible destinations. Which way is up? Or down? One staircase leads to another and leads back to the original staircase. What seems normal, soon becomes inverted. Movies like *Labyrinth*, *Harry Potter*, and *Inception* have portrayed staircases in Escher fashion. What seems impossible, Escher made possible through creativity, mathematics, and pure genius.

Entrepreneurs must be creative, or they become mere copiers of what others have done. So avoid the *copying* trap by seeing what others have done and *create* some better.

An artist's goal is to take viewers on a rewarding journey. The entrepreneur's goal is much the same. Offer a vision that investors would be foolish to ignore.

The analogy of a square peg for a round hole presents an impossible fit. Everybody knows a square peg won't fit a round hole. Who says? I can put a square peg in a round hole if the corners fall within the circumference of the circle. Okay, maybe that's a dumb example, but I'll argue that it's not dumb if it leads to possibility thinking. What do we do when something doesn't fit? Get a bigger hammer. Or maybe there's a better way. The square peg isn't solid but actually a bundle of depressible pins that will conform to any shape hole. What might that idea accomplish?

One of the first rules of creativity is to break the rules. Set aside all the assumptions and allow yourself to consider what's never been considered before. Will it work? I don't know. What will it cost to try it and see? If that doesn't work, it might lead to something that will, which we wouldn't have considered, otherwise.

This is the Art of an Entrepreneur. Seeing ways around conventional ideas, breaking through, and creating something unique.

The Panic Trap

The creative mind can find solutions or workarounds to every problem. Without that creativity, we panic, caught in the *I can't* trap. With creative thinking, we don't panic, quitting too quickly. Instead, we quickly think of every possibility. Then we think of the impossibilities. Next, almost magically, we find a possible solution we hadn't considered, and there's no need to panic.

Elon Musk's journey with Tesla is a powerful story of staying focused under pressure, refusing to panic, and relentlessly pursuing a vision that many thought impossible. In an industry long dominated by fossil-fuel-powered vehicles, Musk faced immense challenges, but he never wavered in his commitment to revolutionize transportation.

In 2008, Tesla was teetering on the brink of collapse, hit hard by the global financial crisis. The company struggled to secure funding. Skepticism from investors in the automotive industry was at an all-time high. Musk, who had already poured much of his personal wealth into Tesla, faced the reality that his bold vision might fail. Instead of panicking, he stayed focused on the goal. He made personal sacrifices, investing his last $35 million into Tesla. He took personal loans to keep the company afloat. At one point, he was living off loans from friends, a testament to his unwavering belief in Tesla's mission.

Despite these dire circumstances, Musk never lost sight of innovation and the long-term goal of making electric vehicles mainstream. Tesla's first car, the Roadster, was more than just a vehicle. It was a statement, proving that electric cars could compete with traditional vehicles in both performance and range. Musk's focus paid off when Tesla secured a crucial $465 million loan from the U.S. Department of Energy, allowing the company to develop the Model S and expand its manufacturing capabilities.

The Model S set new benchmarks for electric vehicles in performance, range, and safety, earning critical acclaim and establishing Tesla as a serious player in the automotive industry. Musk's vision extended beyond just building cars; he was focused on creating an entire ecosystem for electric vehicles, including the Supercharger network and energy storage solutions, which further solidified Tesla's leadership in sustainable transportation.

Elon Musk's story with Tesla is an artistic journey of resilience and the power of staying focused on your goals, no matter the obstacles. By refusing to panic and maintaining a steadfast commitment to his vision, he led Tesla from the brink of failure to becoming a global leader.

Every successful leader has a story of perseverance and pushing through impossible situations. Be the leader. Be the successful person you believe yourself to be. Slow down. Think through the situation and creatively find the solution to your problem.

And keep working to unlock more of your creative genius inside.

Points to Ponder

- Break limiting beliefs: The "this is too hard" trap is a progress killer. Like learning to ride a bike, overcoming fear and doubt is crucial for personal and professional growth.
- Innovate with unconventional thinking: Entrepreneurs need creative minds to break conventional molds that say it can't work and discover how it really can.
- Prepare with realistic foresight: Like the author's swim across the lake, short-sightedness can lead to unnecessary difficulties. Foresight and preparation are key to navigating challenges effectively.

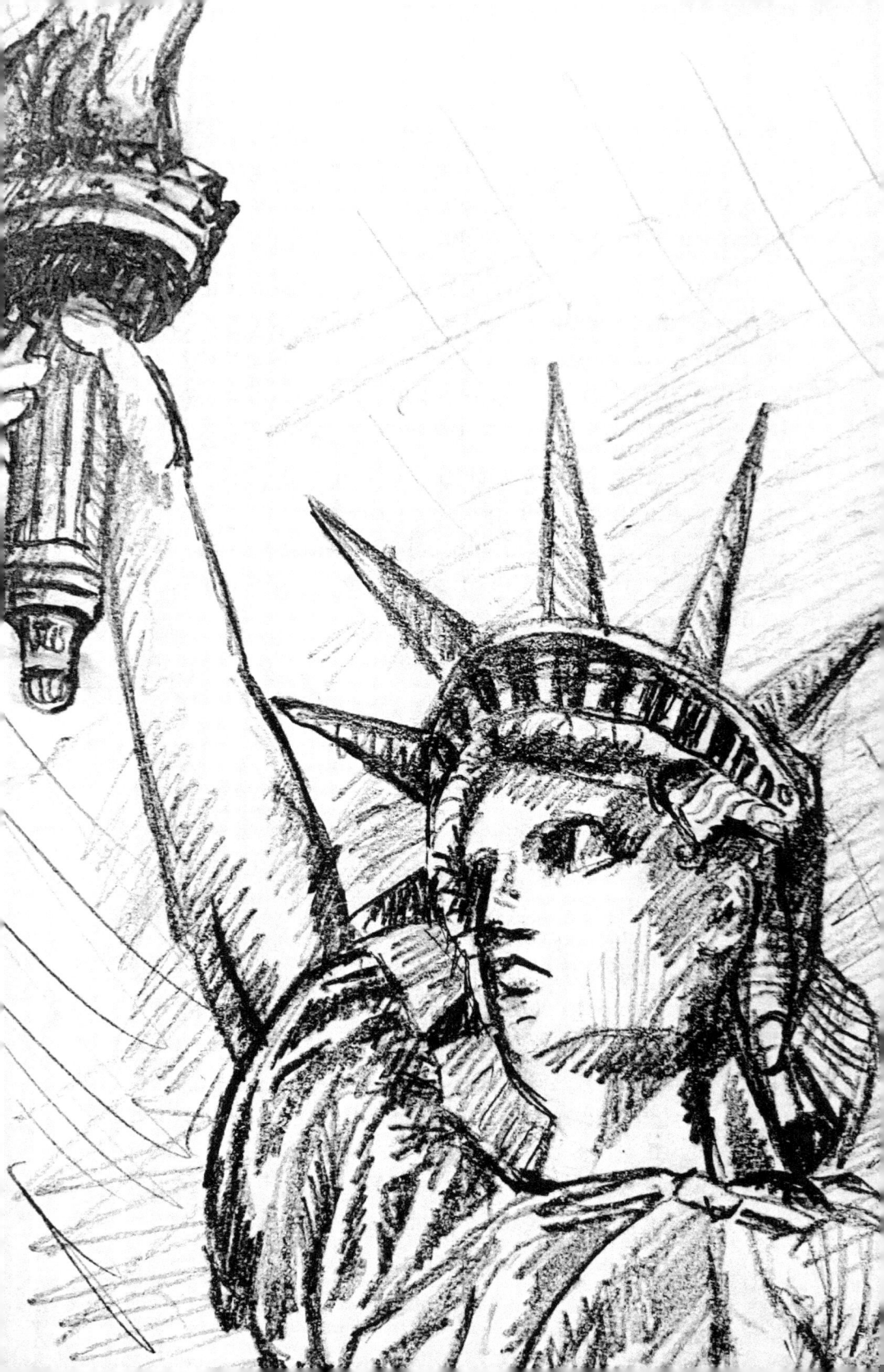

Ideation in the Process

Artistic expressions aren't limited to paint, brush, and canvas any more than musicians are limited to percussion, strings, and horns. As kids, we could build sandcastles, bake mud pies, or invent a game with no more than rocks and sticks. This worked for as long as we weren't convinced that we couldn't color outside the lines or have a purple cow eat pink grass.

We should thank Dr. Seuss for green eggs and ham, the Sneetches, and the Lorax, or growing up would have been colorless and boring. But if we're not careful as adults, we'll have watched Captain James T. Kirk go where no man had gone before but will miss the present opportunities filled with new challenges and exciting adventures.

Lite Brite

Among the top 100 best toys ever made, Lite Brite is a member of the National Toy Hall of Fame. Youngsters could create glowing multicolored pictures with translucent pegs punched through black paper. From flowers to hearts and boats to butterflies, the Lite Brite had endless possibilities for the creative mind. When I flipped on the switch, the colors lit up like a neon sign.

The process began with solid blank paper. What would I create? A ship on the sea. On peg at a time, I used red to show the hull's outline above the water. Blue pegs formed the waterline and the waves. Green defined an island on the horizon, and white put the moon and stars in the sky. After a while, I had an art form that Mom and Dad would admire.

Actually, the process began much earlier, when I opened the box for the first time and didn't have a clue what to do. I started with simple shapes that were included—vehicles, animals, and flowers. This is how the creative process works. We start with copying what others have done, and from that, we imagine something different, something original, created from our own minds.

The business process is much the same. We see what others have done. Then we imagine something different and offer something better than what others have done.

Legos

Building blocks had been around forever, but Lego bricks were one of the hottest toys when I was a kid. No longer was I limited to the two-dimensional art of Lite Brite. I could create houses, skyscrapers, and vehicles in three dimensions. I could even build a train with a motorized engine, rail cars, and track. I was in creative heaven.

Today, children spend hours putting together the most complex objects. Trust me, those children develop creative skills far superior to those who spend their days playing video games. Again, the process of many hours spent on building simple objects leads to original creative complexities.

The creative process is not limited to kids. I have an entrepreneur friend who treats himself with a new Lego set after every win in business. Why? Because the process motivates him and stimulates his creativity to achieve greater levels of success.

Honestly, I have spent my own fair share of time building Legos with my kids, teaching them how each piece fits together to create something out of their imagination.

More than a Picture Puzzle

Building Lego objects is a *process*. You can't just look for a color that matches a spot on the puzzle box picture and find where it fits. With Legos, each piece is placed in relation to the previous piece. First the foundation, then the walls, and finally the roof. Each piece has a specific size, form, place, and purpose. If one piece is misplaced by just one joint, the whole build is messed up.

I soon learned the importance of getting each piece correctly placed to avoid having to start over or backtrack to find where I messed up. That was costly enough, but in business? Better be sure that each step works before going on to the next.

Building Something New

I spent hours with my son building a skyscraper—a true work of art, which he seemed to really appreciate when he took it to his room.

Later, I walked into his room and saw Lego pieces scattered across the floor. "What in the world have you done?" My thumbs were still hurting from all that work.

He looked at me, smiling proudly. "I'm building a pirate ship."

Had my effort been wasted? Not at all, although I thought so, at first. Then I realized that he had learned from my help in building the skyscraper, and now his creativity was leading him to build something of his own. I was proud too.

Sometimes we need to let go of our pride in what we have built and see what others will build on their own for something else, using the same pieces we have used. I would never have thought to build a pirate ship, but my son had. In a similar way, we should be proud of what our employees do, which might be different from what we imagined. And their ideas might become better than our own.

The Lego Movie

I've learned a lot from watching my kids grow up. Otherwise, I might never have watched *The Lego Movie*, an animated movie of a Lego-block world, released in 2014. Some characters, or masters, are able to transform objects into something else—an airplane, for example, needed for escape. The masters find a stash of Legos or another object, and like magic, they start to rearrange the pieces. Until we see it built, we wonder what it will be.

There are countless characters in different scenes, each with a different purpose but essential in this fantasy world. Emmitt falls outside the Lego world and into an external "real" perspective and understand what is happening. However, the movie audience is already aware of this. We now see that this Lego world is the imagination of a child playing with his parents' massive Lego world. The biggest fear of the characters is the Kragle. When we finally see "Kragle," we can see that the label is so worn that we can't see all the letters. We realize that "Kragle" is actually Krazy Glue, and the dad wants to use it to preserve his finished work so it can't be broken apart. The father yells at the child for messing with his Legos and threatens to use the Kragle. The son is heartbroken and finally, the father heart drops, realizing he has stripped imagination and creativity from his son.

Ouch! I saw myself as guilty of the same thing when I forced my son to follow the instructions to build the Millennium Falcon. The big version has over 7,500 pieces, but this was the smaller scale with about 1,400 pieces—a challenge for an eight-year-old, but doable because plastic bags separated groups of pieces for each section of the Falcon. After many hours, he finished and put it on his bookshelf. I was proud because he'd done it without my help.

After a few weeks, I walked into his room, and my prize Millennium Falcon was on the floor, partially dismantled. I freaked. "No! What are you doing?" I was crushed. If I had Kragled it with super glue, the Falcon would still be in one piece.

But no, my son had another idea. He was using the Falcon pieces to build a large base similar to one found on the planet Hoth. Again, I was proud because his imagination and creativity were at work.

As entrepreneurs, we need imaginative, creative employees, those who would find our super-glue commands to be too restrictive.

Building with Success and Failures

As an entrepreneur, I've learned that I may need to break something apart before I have elements needed to build something better. What fit in one place before may now be needed in another place. I may have to get rid of elements and acquire new ones. These are not easy decisions, but they can be crucial for fulfillment of a new vision.

It's okay to try something new. Disassemble the old to produce something new and remarkable. Creativity thrives in the rebuilding process.

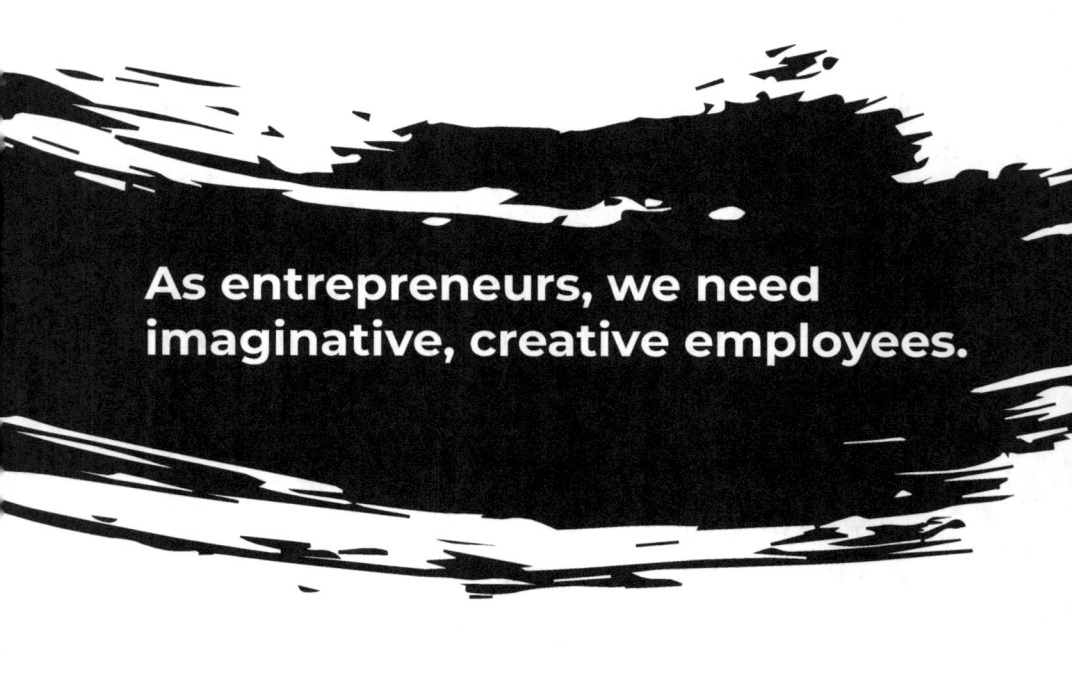

As entrepreneurs, we need imaginative, creative employees.

This reigns true for our company when we review our systems and processes. As a team, we want to make sure every detail is still valid as we continue to grow as a company.

One year, my partner and I were at a conference, frustrated with the process of building a website. Client changes and problems were piling up. There had to be a better way. Honestly, I was bored out of my mind, but the speaker said something that triggered an idea. I immediately grabbed my "napkin" and started to write down this new idea. At the same time, my partner was working on a similar process. When we put them together, magic was achieved.

For our agency, the biggest pain point is client communication and changes—mainly because clients do not always know how to communicate what they want. They don't always know what they really need. With email after email, frustration builds on both sides, potentially damaging the relationship.

In this conference, I was reminded of being called into a client's board room about a logo design. I had designed a new logo and brand for a large company and finalizing it was taking months. It was large enough that they had a committee to make the decision, which always takes longer. In reality, the partners still had the final say.

As I walked into the meeting, I was unsure of what I was getting into. These were powerful, intimidating people. The main partner started to share their concerns about the logo. I listened, took a deep breath, and responded to each concern by addressing them on the big screen. Each time, I explained the reasoning behind the logo design and why their ideas weren't as good. After five minutes, the logo was approved.

Wow! All we needed was five minutes of face-to-face conversation and we were done. I then knew that email was a horrible way to communicate complex thoughts, and this revelation could be foundational in our web development communications.

With my thoughts still churning, I went to work on my "napkin." What if, instead of emails, we had the client come to our office. We could make website changes on the fly, with them in the room. Instead of all the back and forth over weeks, meeting for a day, face-to-face, would give us instant feedback as we built the site.

My partner and I spent the next hour outlining the base premise for our in-person web building process. Instead of taking months to build a site, we could do it in a matter of days. With instant feedback, we would have fewer headaches for both the company and the client, making it a win-win for everyone.

Our plan didn't magically work overnight. We took six months to test, iterate, and dial in the process. After that, we had the core process that would serve well for over a decade. It's one of the key reasons to our longevity.

Let this story be a reminder that revisiting old systems and making them better is a necessity. Do not let yourself become too comfortable with the way things are, because that is a recipe for a competitor to produce something better and leave you wondering what went wrong.

Think about how much more you can achieve if you take time to build something better. Don't be afraid to move forward, because your creative genius will grow through the new ideas and ingenuity you implement. Embrace the Art of an Entrepreneur.

Points to Ponder

- Master the process step-by-step: Like building Lego structures, ensure each business element fits correctly before moving forward.
- Encourage creativity in others: Sometimes leaders must let go of their own ideas to encourage better ideas from employees, just as the author's son re-built his Lego creation into something new.
- Let copying lead to originality: The creative process often starts by imitating others, and then we see how we can build something new and better.

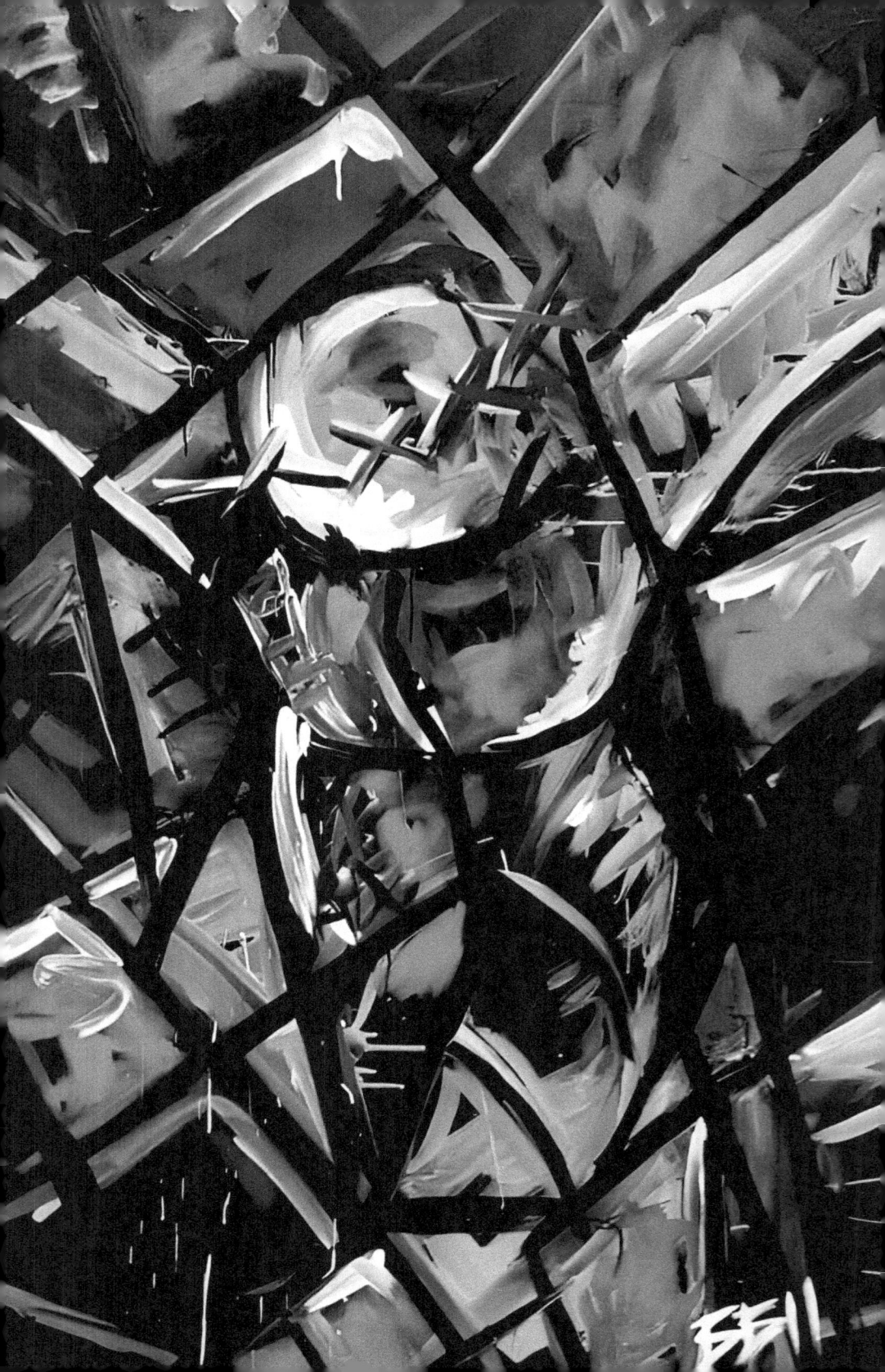

Vision Beyond the Obvious

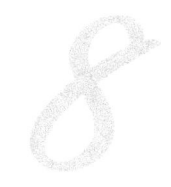

An artist wants to stimulate the viewer with movements of sound, voice, and action—with colors and shapes on a canvas or an actor's expressions, tone, and actions. Music and theater have the same goal: to move people. The same is true for you as an entrepreneur. Unless you motivate people, nothing happens.

You want employees with a passion for excellence. You also want customers to value your products and services because they are vital to the business. Obviously, without customers, we have no revenue to cover expenses and make a profit. For your enterprise to thrive, you must be creative, able to imagine what others want, which doesn't always match what you think they want. Unless their vision supports your effort, the business can't grow.

Consider the proverbial inability to see the forest for the trees. What does that mean? From anywhere in the forest, the view is different. As observers of their forests, supervisors may not see what is obvious to the trees. As the entrepreneur, you may have a vision for the forest, but how can the trees share your vision? Every team and the entire enterprise must share the same vision, or we have the trees competing instead of supporting one another.

Silver Paint

Many of us want a GPS to tell us where we are and give us the next turn, especially when we are lost in the forest. Some prefer to ignore roadmaps and figure everything out on their own, missing some key details hidden right under their own nose.

In pursuit of an art degree during my freshman year of college, I watched another artist present his latest work. Staring at the canvas, I was mesmerized at the detail of the painting and could hardly believe the brilliance of the chrome bowl. I knew of no pigment that could create that effect, so I asked the artist, "What silver paint did you use for the chrome?"

He hesitated, looking puzzled, as if I had just asked a stupid question. Then, as if I was an idiot for asking the question, he laughed and walked away. I can still remember how I felt in that moment.

But was I really an idiot? Apparently, or he would have answered. What was I missing? Choking down my embarrassment, I walked closer to the canvas and inspected the well-placed brush strokes and different colors. Where was the chrome color? A minute passed before I realized it wasn't there. Suddenly, I knew the reason for the artist's puzzled look. From a distance, I saw a realistic polished chrome bowl, but up close, I saw how just the right placement of different pigments worked together to make the bowl appear more real than a chrome bowl on my kitchen counter.

Chrome wasn't a color. It was like a mirror projecting the light and color of its surroundings. The lemon next to the bowl was a mere reflection that followed the curvature of the bowl. If I were to place something else next to the bowl, the colors and highlights would change. It was at this moment that my eyes opened to a whole new world.

The perspectives from which we see our worlds makes all the difference. Up close, the details and colors were clear. From a distance, they blended and presented an entirely different picture. As an entrepreneur, you deal with the same principle. From a distance, the issues appear to be one thing. But up close, you'll find something remarkably different.

You have the big picture on where the business is going. Others are the paint, brushstrokes, piano keys, or guitar strings that produce the finished product. In the opening of your artistic mind, you will find true vision for being an entrepreneur.

The Spoon

Opening the mind goes beyond just seeing paint or colors on a canvas. In *The Matrix* movie, the main character Neo goes to see a woman known as the Oracle. It was believed she could confirm whether Neo was "The One" destined to end the war between humans and machines. As he enters her apartment, Neo encounters a young boy holding a spoon that bends and straightens as if the boy is bending it with his mind. Neo is given the spoon, but nothing happens. Confused, trying to discover the mystery, the boy says, "Do not try to bend the spoon. That's impossible. Instead, only try to realize the truth."

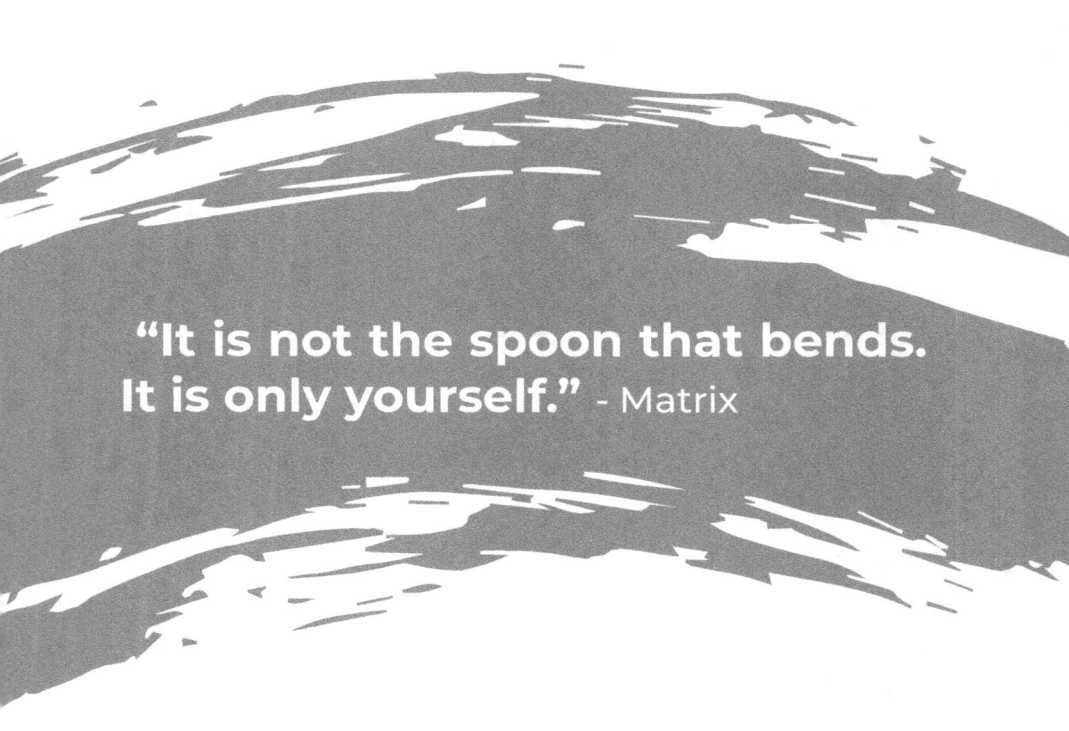

> ## "It is not the spoon that bends. It is only yourself." - Matrix

Wait. He's holding the spoon. Why shouldn't he try to bend the spoon? How is bending the spoon impossible? He has the strength, doesn't he? No, the boy said it was impossible. What was he not seeing? "What truth?" he asks.

"There is no spoon," the boy says. "It is not the spoon that bends. It is only yourself."

Holding the spoon before his eyes, Neo stares intensely and sees from a new perspective. The spoon moves and bends, then straightens.

The reality we see is the only reality we know. Some say that seeing is believing. Maybe so, but it's equally true, if not more so, that what we see is determined by what we believe. By believing the impossible, we can see the impossible as possible and know how to do it. In *The Matrix* movie, the spoon wasn't *really* a spoon, was it? In Neo's mind, it was, and that's the point.

The spoon is an object. When you see it as more than you thought it was, it can blur, bend, straighten, or become something else. Does the spoon bend? Yes, in your mind, and that perspective makes all the difference.

In business, we think we see reality. But do we, really? Take another look. What are you missing? It's there, but you didn't notice. You assume people want something and why, but that's based on your knowledge, thoughts, and feelings. Their reality is different, and that can be an opportunity or obstacle depending on what you see.

Take a moment and think of what you are facing right now. Are the circumstances taking you toward where you want to be? What's holding you back? If you saw it before, you would have done something about it. Keep looking until the possibilities become real in your mind. Only then can they be real in your actions.

In a mastermind event, Ryan Deiss spoke about his evolution as a business leader. He had growing businesses with several points of leadership and related jobs. The business growth caused a major shift in his daily routine, but he never knew he was holding on to the spoon. His businesses grew to the point he had to let go, so he interviewed applicants and hired the right workers.

Entrepreneurs want to manage the enterprise, giving it direction and assuring its health, but not be a worker *in* the business. So they are constantly looking to train their replacements. As many times as they can work themselves out of one job, they gain a promotion to satisfy a greater need, and more people benefit.

Ryan reached the point where he wasn't needed in specific day-to-day operations, but this was where he excelled. Much of his self-worth came doing the work and setting an example for others. He had qualified people to do that work, but he didn't want to let go of the spoon. So, he found projects or issues where he could be the savior and fix the problems, proving his value.

Stepping away wasn't easy. He had to visualize the spoon differently and see that he was hindering the business by not releasing responsibilities to others. The business could only scale so much if he continued to sabotage the business to prove his self-worth. He knew the employees could do the work, but he had to let go so they could do it. Let them make mistakes just like he had done. If they needed help, he was there. But otherwise, he had more-important things to do.

Successful entrepreneurs like Ryan will tell you to hire people who are smarter and better than you are. The hard part can be accepting that they really are better. But in doing so, you are free to see what others don't see and can share vision that will lead the business in future growth.

A "spoon" in business can take various forms. It represents whatever is distracting you from being all you can be. Your goal is to see beyond the spoon and realize there is no spoon at all. Sure, the issues you deal with are important. But they aren't what keeps you from reaching your goals.

What are you doing to push your thought process? Your artistic brain is much more capable than you might imagine—if you will push yourself outside your comfort zone.

Which Way Is Up?

Moving beyond your comfort zone can be hard. When I was growing up, I preferred to stay home and play sports or video games. My workaholic dad left for work so early and came home so late that we didn't get to spend much time together. The best way for me to spend time with him was to spend time with him at work. As a teenager during the summer, I would go to enjoy some one-on-one lunches. Wonderful!

One day at lunch, I noticed something unusual about his watch. The hour and minute hands on the clock face were upside down from what I expected. Why? Upon closer inspection, I realized that the watch was right-side-up for me, the same as if I were seeing a clock on the wall. But when he glanced at his wrist, the hour hand was close to six o'clock, not noon. From his perspective, the watch was upside down, which made no sense.

I looked at my watch, then looked at his. "Why is your watch upside down?"

He smiled. "It's right side up for you. Why did you even notice?"

Good question, because I didn't have an answer. Why had I noticed?

He had to explain. "Subconsciously, you expected the hour hand to be where it would normally be, but it wasn't there, was it? That got your attention, and you realized that it was on the exact opposite side. In a fraction of a second, your brain said, *Dad's watch is upside down.* Right?"

I nodded. "But why?"

"Brain testing," he said.

"I don't understand."

"Our brains are capable of more than we can imagine, but the way we see things must be challenged, or we can miss seeing even the obvious. I read about a university study where test students were given special goggles that made them see everything upside-down. After wearing those goggles 24/7 for several days, they saw everything right-side-up. And for a moment after taking the goggles off, everything was upside down."

"Interesting," I said, but what does that have to do with your watch?"

"That's the way creativity works. One thought leads to another if we're asking what-if questions and using our imaginations. I wondered, *What would happen if I wore my watch upside down. How long would it take for me to see it right-side-up?* I'd never know if I didn't try it."

Amazing. As old as I thought my dad was, his schooling hadn't squelched his creativity. I wanted to be like that, but could I? Maybe he was just more talented, and naturally creative. "You can just glance at your watch and see what time it is, even though it's upside-down? How long did it take to learn how?"

"That's the amazing thing about our minds. Ask it a question and give it awhile—maybe a day or two. At some point, it will give you an answer, or at least suggest possibilities that lead to more what-if questions."

"Yeah, but you didn't answer my question."

"You're right. For the first day or two, I twisted my head a bit so I could see what time it was. But it was like those university students with upside-down goggles but soon saw everything right-side-up. After a few days, I forgot that my watch was upside-down. I just glanced down and saw what time it was."

I thought he was teaching his mind to do new things. In a way, that's true, I guess. But more specifically, he continually challenged his brain with possibilities, asking it questions, testing its capability. I thought he was smart, but actually, he was enjoying his childlike ignorance to discover what the average person would never imagine.

Like father, like son. If he could be creative, I could too. He helped me believe that, or I might never have known that all brains are hardwired to be creative. We just need to keep it stimulated with possibilities.

A few years later, I noticed his watch. "You're still wearing your watch upside-down. Why?"

"I'm more comfortable with it this way," he said. "I did try another test."

"Really?" I couldn't imagine what test that could be. He had done the brain test and found the answer. What more could he want to know? "What kind of test?"

"I wondered what would happen if I turned my watch right-side-up on even-numbered days and upside-down on odd-numbered days. Would my brain be so confused that it couldn't tell what time it was? Nope. After a couple of weeks, somehow I was always aware of the date, whether it was an odd or even number, so when I glanced at my watch, I just saw it right-side-up, no matter which way it was turned."

"But today is an *even* day, and the watch is upside down."

"It was too much trouble switching it back and forth in the mornings, so I just leave it upside-down all the time. Sometimes, people notice it's upside-down, and that stirs an interesting conversation about creativity."

Imagination can see things upside down, right side up, or inside-out—in ways that are not physically possible. Our creative minds are full of artistic ideas that only need to be unlocked through the idea of possibility.

Walk in the Park

Years later, I was married and had three kids when my dad decided an early morning walk would do him good. Each day, no matter the weather, he left his upstairs apartment, walked three blocks to the park, and followed the circular path clockwise around the pond. He counted the number of times around the pond, increasing the number until he was walking at least a mile.

After a year, he wondered how it would feel to walk around that pond the same as he had always done, but this time go counterclockwise. The feeling was different. As he made the circle, the fishing dock was on his left, not the right. The privacy fences of the neighbors were on his right, not his left. But that wasn't all that was different. Why hadn't he noticed the tree on the right, the one with all the wild grapevines. The brush and tall grass on his left didn't look the same. Why? Instead of seeing it from the south, he was looking from the north. That day, he noticed a dozen differences that he'd never noticed before, even though he'd walked that path countless times.

Like everybody else, he was a "creature of habit," going the same way every day. Some call this process a "routine" or maybe being "in the groove." But I think he would call it "being in a rut." He'd grown comfortable in his ways, almost forgetting what it would be like to do something different, just for the fun of it, just to see what the change would be like. Instead of going the same way to the store, he went another way and saw thing he'd never seen before. But that wasn't all.

His walk in the parks reminded him to pay better attention. Why was that boy sitting on the park swing? It was a school day. He challenged his imagination. Evidently, when Mom dropped him at school and drove away, he walked toward the park instead of the school building. Dad was training his brain to heat up his imagination, which he'd allowed to grow cold. In his mind, he saw the boy entering the school just before lunch, happy to have missed the exam in his English class. Would he enjoy lunch? No, it wasn't pizza day.

When was the last time you used your imagination to create a story as real as a downpour that made you wish for an umbrella? Growing up, you used your imagination to make sense of the world around you. When we don't exercise that ability as adults, we make too many assumptions. We don't see what's around the next corner, because we didn't think to look that way. That can be costly, even fatal, in business because of what "you never saw coming."

Let's make this practical. The next time you need to open up your mind to new things in your business, you might enjoy a walk in the park. The break will allow your brain to recharge and focus on the things you might be missing. You can retrain your mind and pay attention to important things you would otherwise miss.

Understanding the walk-in-the-park benefits, Lucasfilm built Skywalker Ranch to foster creativity and imagination outside the office. The serene landscapes encouraged relaxation, while the state-of-the-art resources stimulated imaginative thinking, making it a powerful catalyst for overcoming normal creative blocks and revitalizing artistic expression.

Speedreading

At times, I would much rather be in a place like Skywalker Ranch, enhancing my creativity. But at other times, I need to be learning as much as I can. The hard part about learning and being a creative is that your mind doesn't easily shut off. It can wander from thought to thought, word to word, and then you forget what you just read.

If you watch people reading silently in a bookstore or library, you will often see their lips moving. Why do they do that?

When we first learned to read, we had to say the words aloud so the teacher or a parent knew we were seeing the word and correctly translating text to speech. That process hard-wired our brains to read at about the same rate that we talk: 120–150 words per minute. We can think much faster than we talk, but if we vocalize the words in our minds, the mental process must slow down.

Some people believe they must read slowly to fully grasp the meaning, but that's not always true. Suppose you were speeding down the freeway at 30 mph—because the engine had a problem, and you couldn't go any faster. Would you then see more? In five minutes, you'd see 2.5 miles of road ahead, right? Yes, the math is right, but the truth is, you'd pay little attention to the road or where you're going. You'd mostly hear honking and cars zipping past you. But what if you were driving at 90 mph? In five minutes, you've covered three times the distance, and you're 100 percent focused on what's ahead. Speedreading is something like that. To read faster, you have to focus, quickly seeing the sentence and grasping its meaning because you're desperate to get the picture and move forward in the shortest possible time.

Nobody learns to drive at 90 mph. They start from zero and move up from there as their conscious practices create subconscious neural pathways that process a thousand times faster. What factors limit how fast you can drive? Traffic. Speed limits. Road conditions. The weather. And our driving skills. Given the conditions, people usually choose a comfortable speed. Racecar drivers can be comfortable at 120 mph weaving in and out of traffic.

Years ago, my dad had very little free time for reading and research. He needed to read a book in an hour, not days or weeks. So he bought a copy of *The Evelyn Wood Seven-Day Speed Reading and Learning Program*, which promised to double his reading speed by the end of the book—if he did all the exercises. That method was strange, insisting he could rapidly follow the line with his finger, read alternate lines from right to left, and still comprehend what was written. Sure enough, with practice, his brain adjusted to seeing and understanding the whole line instead of just one word at a time. At the first exercise in the book, he read at about 200 wpm. By the end of the book, he was amazed—right at 400 wpm.

He kept trying to push his speed, but he didn't feel like he was getting much better. As luck would have it, he noticed an ad for an all-day speedreading seminar at a local hotel, so he signed up. At the beginning of the day, the first speed test had him reading 380 wpm with 30 percent comprehension. Not bad, except for the comprehension part. But to be honest, his comprehension probably wasn't that good at slower speeds, either. On the last test of the day, he was at 750 wpm and 80 percent comprehension. *Now that's better*, he thought.

How could he have gone twice as fast, and at the same time, have 2.67 times better comprehension? There was only one explanation. Like driving 90 mph instead of 30, he had intensified his focus and concentration. The seminar instructor said to him, "If you don't keep practicing this, you'll lose it." So every day, he pushed himself until he could read 100 pages of familiar material in five minutes. He spent fifteen minutes a day reading the Bible. By the end of each month, he had read the whole Bible cover-to-cover. Amazing? He doesn't think so. He says our subconscious minds are capable of seeing a page in a second and know what it says—a process called *photo reading*. He bought the course but never learned how, because he was comfortable with driving at variable speeds based on a book's content, style, and what he wanted to know. He says watching a movie can be difficult because it moves so slow. For him, speedreading a novel is like watching a movie at double-speed while seeing and hearing everything that happens.

I don't speedread, but I have done speed-painting. I once painted some great works of art on canvases that were 8 ft x 8 ft. I had to paint them on a church stage during one song—in just 5 minutes and 33 seconds. Before that day, I'd had lots of practice on smaller pieces, but with at least triple the time allotted. In this short time on a canvas that was as tall as I could reach, there wasn't time to contemplate. I had to paint without conscious forethought.

In football, many college quarterbacks struggle transitioning to the professional level because the game moves so much faster. It is normal to hear professional quarterbacks say the game slows down after about three years. In truth, the game doesn't really slow down. With three years of intensely focused experience, their mental processes speed up.

Also, professional baseball players can hit a home run when the ball is fired across the plate at 100 mph. There's no time to think. Simultaneous with the ball leaving the pitcher's hand, the bat must begin its motion across the plate, or the bat could not possibly contact the ball when it reaches the plate. How does that happen? Batters practice every day since Little League—until their posture, position, grip, and swing happen without conscious thought.

From a business perspective, as in the big leagues, you might want to intensify your focus on what matters most. Okay, slow down for a moment and consider what skill you have neglected for lack of time. Intensify your focus. Be creative. And practice, practice, practice until you're comfortable with faster speeds.

Imagine the impact to your business if you were able open your eyes and see more clearly than you've ever seen before. In the process, expand your vision by giving yourself the ability to slow down enough to embrace creativity. Then challenge yourself to push beyond existing boundaries to learn new techniques and launch a whole new outlook. A fresh perspective on business can lead to greater success. Your art is just beginning and will continue to thrive as you continue this journey.

Points to Ponder

- See the big picture: The "seeing the forest for the trees" metaphor reminds us to balance details (trees) with the broad vision (forest) to align teams and avoid conflicting goals.
- Perspectives matter: Entrepreneurs must continually examine situations from different viewpoints to uncover hidden realities and possibilities.
- Practice leads to mastery: Like quarterbacks and baseball players, we sharpen our entrepreneurial skills by relentless practice and study of the game.

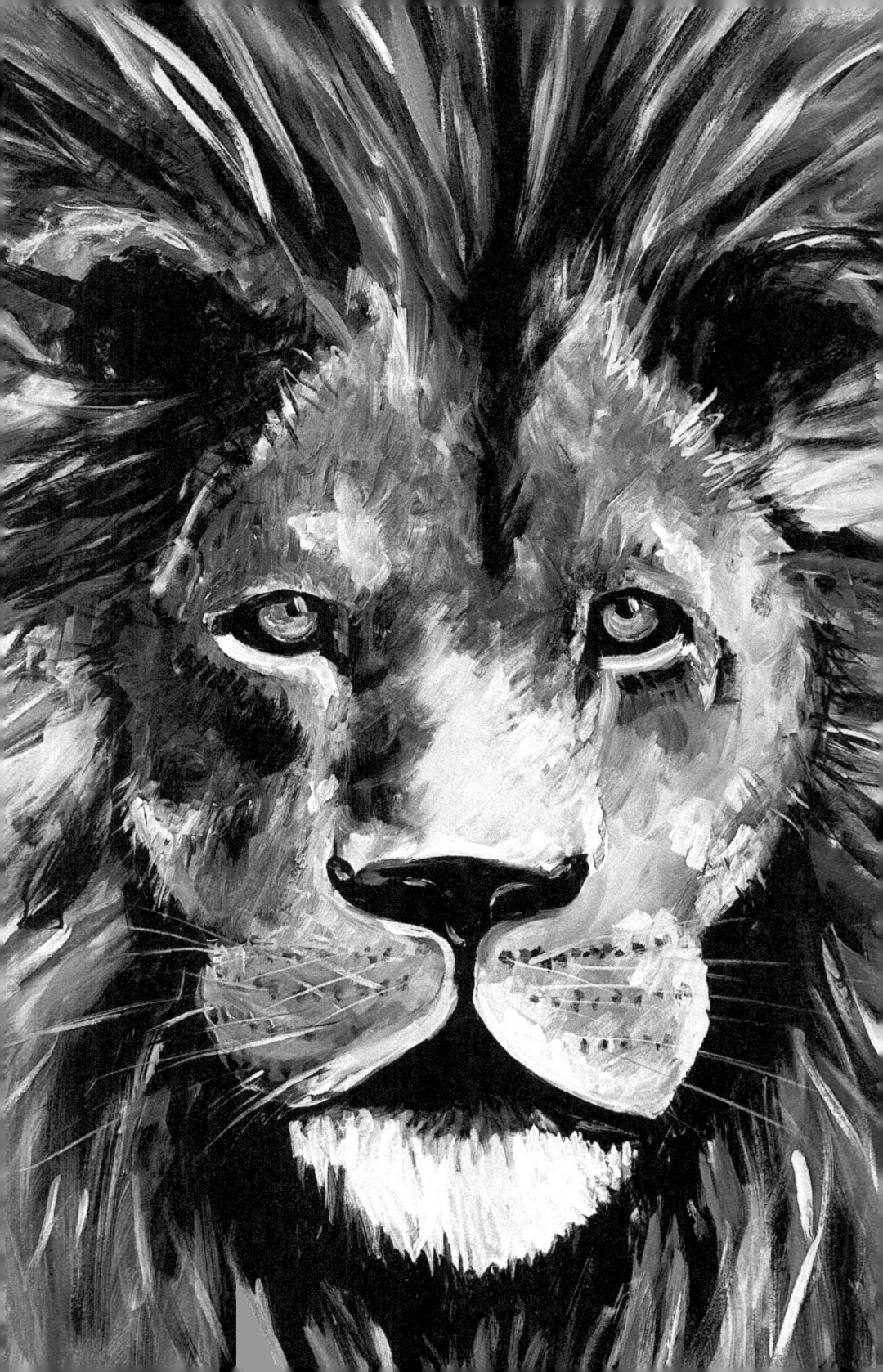

The Lost Art of Wonder and Play

Without a doubt, children are full of creativity and wonder. What happened to us as adults? Why did we lose our creativity? The truth is, we never lost it. We were put into an environment where we were not allowed to practice it.

Days When We Were Young

At the height of your creativity and imagination, you could ask questions, explore, and enjoy your surroundings. You played for endless hours—but that ended when you started school. At least we got to play during recess, but not when you got to middle school. Then it was all study and no play. We were expected to accept without question everything we were taught.

We still needed exercise, didn't we? Running and playing all day was no longer an option. No problem. Physical education classes gave us exercise, but those periods provided no opportunity to freely ask questions and explore new ideas. There were still rules never to be broken. *Maximum effort* was alive and well. That was the goal. But *creativity* was almost dead because of "the desk."

Tied to a Desk

Weekday classes run from roughly from 8:00 a.m. to 3:00 p.m. Other than P.E. and going between sessions, you're sitting at a desk. Think about all the time we spend sitting—on the ride to and from school, at the dinner table, while watching TV, when playing video games or texting. We may be seeing *pictures* of the world around us, but to experience it, we need to get out more.

Like youngsters who could run and play all day, now we must pursue activities with a purpose. What is that? First, avoid being tied to a desk most of the day. I love the story of young Johnny who was told to sit down and be quiet. The teacher asked why he was grinning from ear to ear. "I may be sitting down on the inside," he said, "but I'm still standing on the inside." What's the point? The chair represents being tied to a daily routine, without the freedom to even think about breaking out to be creative.

But if you want to be creative, you can, no matter where you are or what you're doing. You are not limited to the desk where you are assigned. Get up and enjoy creative freedom.

Path to Imagination and Creativity

In school, I saw creativity encouraged only in my art classes. I loved to bring stories to life in pictures on paper. In the eighth grade, an art class was required. We tend to excel at what we like, and art was no exception. My teacher suggested I apply for the select class in the next school year, so I submitted my portfolio and was accepted.

In the ninth grade, I sat among some amazing students and saw myself in a competitive environment where I couldn't possibly win. I did okay, but I felt like a loser, which was the perfect attitude for quitting. Playing football and baseball had become my main focus. In the tenth grade, a scheduling conflict was a great excuse to walk away from art altogether. Fortunately, I worked out the schedule, and a flicker of hope burst into a creative flame that refused to die.

From that point, I focused on creativity and art. Thirty years later, I still remember many of those art projects. One week, I had to turn in a watercolor from one of the theme options, in this case an "underwater giraffe on acid." Think about that. A giraffe underwater was easy enough to visualize. I pictured bubbles rising out of its nose and bursting on the surface. But what about "on acid"? I saw vibrant colors mixed with blue shades of water, something psychedelic.

Like everybody else, my work had to be posted for class critique, which was scary at first. The best was displayed all week for all the classes to see. I soon learned that failure was a prerequisite for success, because some of my work was not great but beauty really was in the eye of the beholder. At times, I was chosen when I didn't think I'd done my best work—but the giraffe, it was one of my best.

In previous failures, I learned what made a great piece of art and what didn't. Through trial and error, I became better and better at my craft. Knowing the exhilaration of being chosen was second to none as a young artist. I was hooked and challenged myself to step out and do new things.

Iceberg Invincibility

You probably know what sunk the *Titanic*, a luxury ship that was supposedly invincible. Most people think an iceberg caused the tragedy, but it was much more than that. *Failure to see beneath the surface* was the bigger problem.

Ice floats, but that doesn't mean an iceberg is sitting *on top* of the water. Only a little shows above the surface. Most of it hides beneath the surface, about 90 percent, to be more precise. Your creative ability is much like that, something to be avoided when it doesn't conform to already established formulas for success. Exposed, it might sink your ship. But let it stay hidden, and you'll never know what impossibilities you might make possible, just because you had a radical idea that nobody had considered before.

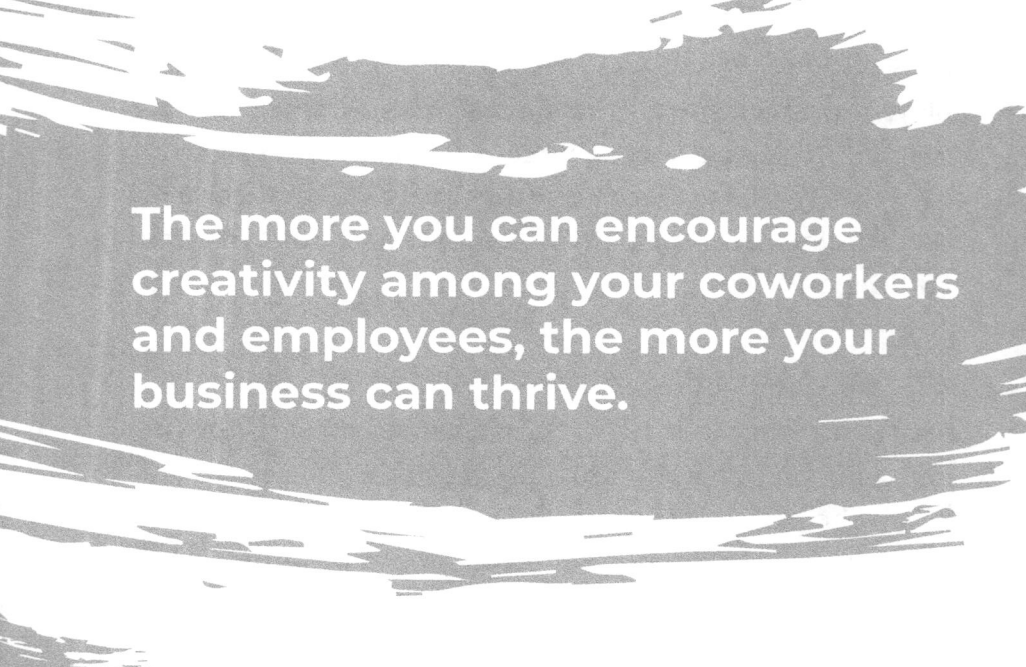

The more you can encourage creativity among your coworkers and employees, the more your business can thrive.

The more you embrace your creative self as a top-shelf entrepreneur, the more impact you will have on your surroundings—at work, at home, and at play. But the opportunity doesn't end there. The more you can encourage creativity among your coworkers and employees, the more your business can thrive.

Imagine 90 percent of your team's potential hidden below the surface. What if you could enhance or pull out a fraction of that potential? It would completely change your business, wouldn't it? But you must see it and then call it out of your team, because it is what great leaders do.

Musical Painting

It takes a leader to see what is below the surface. In 1997, my friend Ben Pasley had produced a Christian music album with the group 100 Portraits and wanted to do something different for the album release. I saw him as a talented and unusually creative musician who was most appreciative of all art forms. He approached me with his vision for the concert—to bring the arts back into the church. He wanted to combine music, art, and dance in a church event.

Wow! That sounded amazing.

Ballet wasn't necessarily my idea of Christian worship, but with his music, it was an amazing combination. Some churches only had an organ. That's all. But these were modern times when we could allow guitars and drums in church. But an orchestra? Strobe lights? And dancers? We were talking about a *church* event, not theater. What could be better than just playing samples of his music?

Ben asked if I would paint on stage during the concert and only paint whatever I was feeling as the music was played. He wanted a dancer to move as she felt led by the melodic sounds. No preplanning. No conductor to direct our movements. The dancer would dance, and the painter would paint. And the musicians would do what musicians do. Simple. But weird. His creativity was showing way above the waterline, but he also saw what was below the surface in my own life and creativity.

Shared Creativity

Ben was a leader, and I was being led into a venture I'd never considered before. This is something that all of us, as leaders, need to understand. Giving people opportunities to be creative is crucial as they work to accomplish their goals. Otherwise, we hinder success and don't know what we've missed. Neither do they.

If Ben hadn't shared his vision, I would have missed much of my potential. Given the challenge, I had to stand on stage with a large canvas. In a matter of minutes instead of days, I was to paint something that would inspire his audience. How?

Suppose you as a leader share a vision, something you want others to accomplish. They have the skills. You don't. You have a goal in mind, but you're not the "painter." They are. How can you challenge them to add their creative capability to what they would normally do and accomplish something spectacular? Encouraging the spectacular will propel your enterprise past the competition.

Speed Painting

Ben's call to get up and do something different led me to become one of the first, if not the very first, speed painters in the world. Even today, I know of only a handful of artists who do what I call "speed painting" before a live audience. Most artists need time for planning, sketching different aspects of the work, and doing preliminary drawings. When they finally get to put the first brush stroke on the canvas, they may need many weeks to see every detail in its perfect place.

Speed painting takes practice because so many lengthy thought processes must form in a matter of seconds, and then something is sure not to go right. Then another level of creativity is called for, on-the-spot, because there's no way to undo what's already been done. I have to build on my mistake as if it were something intended.

You may have heard the saying: "Practice makes perfect." Actually, bad practice can make good skills worse— unless we're learning from our mistakes, constantly striving to do better. In that case, the more mistakes, the better. Doing something well takes lots of practice and many mistakes. Whether it's sports, working, or speaking, in music, painting, and even typing, the more you do it with a desire to improve, the better you'll get.

Destructive Distractions

As an entrepreneur, I easily get distracted and spend too much time on daily business tasks instead of creativity. For years, I did the creative work that employees are now responsible for. I had to become the manager, not the chief designer. Meaning: I had to get out of my seat and into a different one.

Transitioning from working in the business to leading the business was difficult. The need for creativity changed from doing the creative work to managing the creative direction for others. I had to learn how to creatively *encourage* the creative skills of others without restricting their productivity. Yet I was most familiar with how to *do* the work, not how to *manage*. I couldn't let routine work distract me from managing.

If I don't do something to stir my own creativity, managing the details of work can also be a distraction. Hand-eye coordination, technique, and creativity can quickly fade when ignored. I grew up playing video games. I know, what a waste of time, right? Well, for me it was a time to unwind or accomplish challenges within the game. As a graphic designer, I design long documents and set up tabs and bullets. My coworker even called me "game-boy hands" because I would quickly hit the keys to rapidly set up the various lines of text. Much like a speed typist whose fingers fly across the keys without looking, my hand-eye coordination let me produce pages and pages of content in record time.

Use It, or Lose It

For over a year, I didn't play one video game. I had more-important things to do. That was fine until I noticed that I felt different. I noticed normal things felt slower, and I was taking longer to create a long document. I started playing some games again and confirmed my suspicion: the decline was due to me not practicing hand-eye coordination.

I have noticed the same thing with my art. When I go long periods of time between paintings, I lose a little comfort and confidence. Without practice, my style can quickly fade. My least favorite art pieces came for lack of practice and preparation.

When your mind is in the right place, you can achieve great things and its practice and preparation that will put your mind in the right place.

Stirring Creative Potential

There is no way around it. You must plan time to practice and stimulate your creativity. Set a date on your calendar and force yourself to do it. Otherwise, distractions will set in, regardless. Even during the process of creating this book, there were days I blocked time to solely focus on this project. As any entrepreneur will tell you, there will always be a fire to put out or something else to be done. You cannot let those things deter you from reaching your full creative potential.

Off and Running

If Ben Pasley had not presented the idea and challenged me to paint on stage, I would never have known what I had missed. Sometimes, we must force ourselves out of our comfortable seats.

Maybe you need to get out more. See what others are doing. Be creative and try something new. Practice old skills that have become rusty from lack of use.

The journey reflects who you are, but it should also challenge you to become more. By unlocking your creative potential with practice and persistence, you embrace the Art of Entrepreneurs. It's time to unlock your creative genius.

Points to Ponder

- Tap into unseen potential: Much like an iceberg, most creative potential lies beneath the surface, which says we must dive deep to see what opportunities lie hidden.
- Embrace new challenges: Like the author's experience with speed painting, try something different. Your key to growth comes from taking risks and stepping beyond your comfort zones.
- Break free from the constraints of routines: Overcome physical limitations and allow space for exploration, play, and thinking beyond the ordinary.

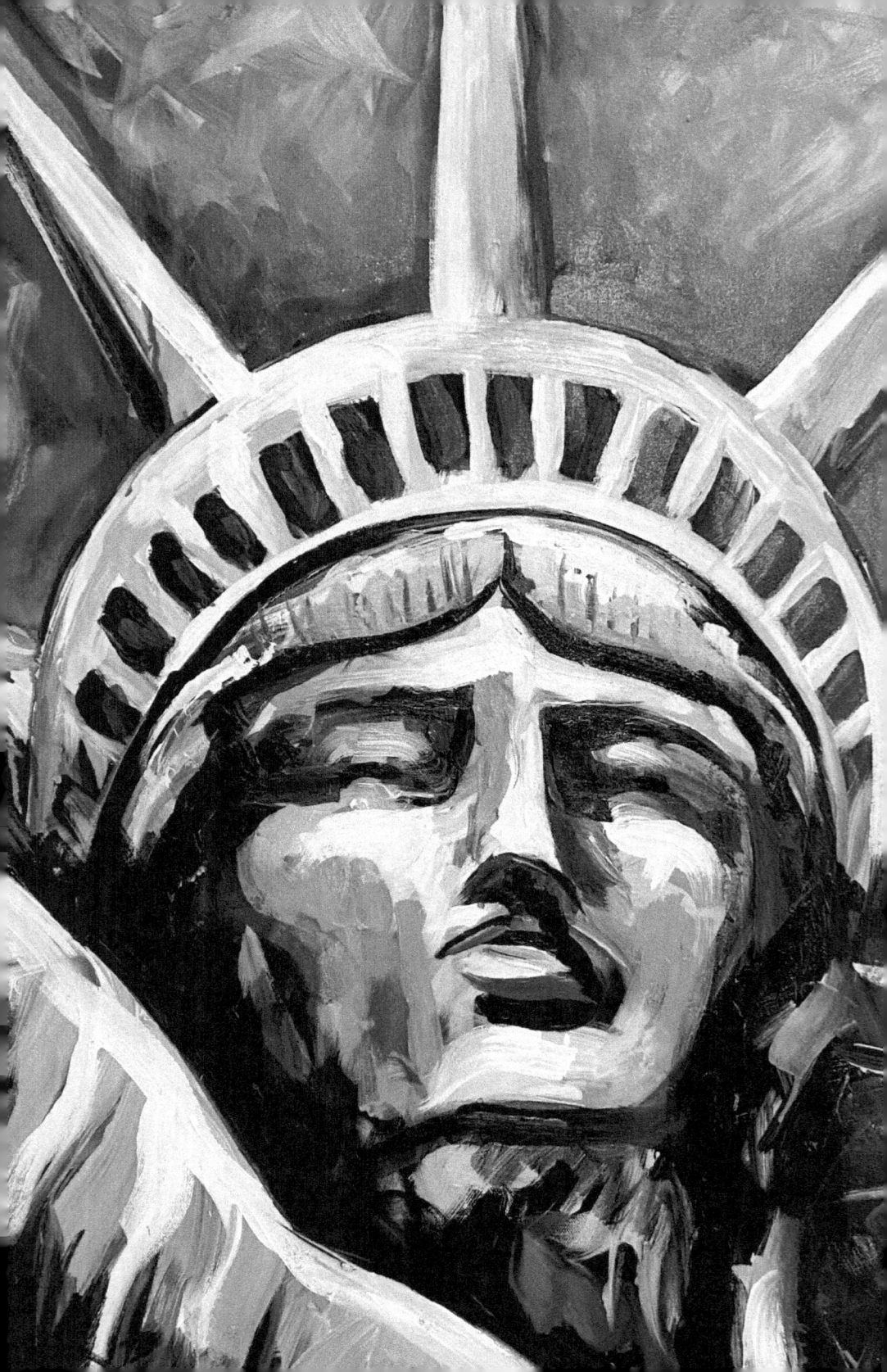

Chasing
Bold
Ideas

Every great entrepreneur is a great thinker. Now that we've considered the blank canvas, it's time to apply creative thinking to your business strategy. The more time and effort spent thinking through processes, goals, and outcomes, the greater your chances of success.

Most entrepreneurial success is not luck. It is well thought out, strategized, and then implemented. It's truly a work of art.

Strategic Focus

In our business, the more we focused and strategized, the more success was created. When we were several individuals doing a job, we were successful, but our growth wasn't sustainable.

As soon as we took a serious look at where we were, where we wanted to be, and how we were going to get there, we saw remarkable improvement. This shift began with exponential thinking.

For as long as we were content with being a six-figure business, we lacked the motivation to become much more. And that's a problem because stagnation should be a life-and-death concern. Society and the marketplace are continually changing. "Good enough" soon becomes "not good enough," and eventually "we're dying" as other businesses pass us by.

How much more could you do if your business doubled in size? What if it doubled again? And again? What happens if the industry changes? Every entrepreneur has different goals in mind. You just need to be aware that thinking smaller will miss the opportunities that exponential thinking might create.

When we had seven employees, we weren't sure if we wanted twelve. Managing people can be hard, and twenty seemed like too many. As we began to define our BHAG (Big Hairy Audacious Goal), having twelve to fifteen employees was difficult to imagine. It might be difficult, but to reach our goals, it was a small hurdle in exponential thinking.

Developing Delegation

We had to think differently, delegating the responsibilities that we had assumed could only be done right if we did the work ourselves. I personally had to abandon my misconception that "if you want something done right, you do it yourself."

As an artist, I was the creative mind behind the ideas. I thought it took "me" to ensure the project was going succeed. But how could I delegate what I *knew* I had to do for the business to succeed? I had to change my mindset, and the change took years because I knew I was "right." I had to do all this stuff myself. But there was another option. A shift to train others with all the knowledge and expertise I had, but also to empower them. Empowering is key and that took time.

Our small team of employees had to be empowered to grow with their own experiences and perspectives to the point that I was no longer needed. This meant a project's success or failure no longer fell upon my focus but the team lead on the project. I anticipated a severely damaged ego, as if I would be totally worthless. But actually, the opposite happened. Now, I was worth more because I could do so much more, and I was really proud of our employees because they could do so much more. Talk about a win-win. This was it.

Training with a Goal in Mind

Empowering people is a lot easier when they are properly trained. Training people to do what they don't need to do makes no sense. Some businesses are sucked into training programs that consume employees' valuable time without a corresponding benefit. The cost doesn't matter, whether it's a thousand dollars or a million. The question is whether the benefit exceeds the cost. If it does, you've made a wise investment that ultimately costs you nothing. It *made* money.

Training is crucial, because you do not want the business to revolve around you. As we targeted growth, I trained two key people to take on many of the daily roles I was handling. Both were amazing, and I trusted them completely.

Many people can become entrepreneurial thinkers who wind up running their business within the security, vision, and growth of our business. I'd love to have more employees with this capability, so they need to be trained with the freedom to be the creative thinkers that they want to be. The more they learn, the more they will help grow the business without my direct involvement.

For a deeper look into thinkers and implementers, take a serious look at Gino Wickman's books *Traction* or *Rocket Fuel*. Most entrepreneurs are "visionaries" and thinkers, but early in their businesses they are often caught having to do everything.

The more your business grows, the more you must delegate. This means that young "entrepreneurs" within your enterprise must also learn to delegate. Otherwise, you are caught in the rat race and never given the opportunity to truly grow.

The Right People in the Right Place

When we parted ways with Daniel, we learned from our mistakes but also owned up to them, as well. As I continued to pick up the pieces from the termination, there was one person we wanted to hire. He was a designer who worked for one of our clients and would have been a great fit with our team, but the situation was awkward because he was friends with Daniel too. He declined working with us and we had to move on.

A year later, we still wanted him to work with us. We knew it wouldn't work it out, because he had left our client and went to work for Daniel's creative agency.

Another year later, we were having lunch with Daniel, who now had another company besides the creative agency. MusicBed was thriving to the point that the agency business had become a burden and a distraction. The agency was overwhelmed because it was a two-person shop with Paul having to do almost everything.

When one person is doing everything, growth is next

to impossible and burnout is almost certain. With so much work that has to be done right now, there is no time left to hire and train. Even if you did, you're still so buried in work that you're left with insufficient management time. You probably have seen this situation before: There isn't enough time to do what's needed to free up time for what's more important but can't do.

We asked, "Could we talk to Paul about working with us?" It was a bold question that could have ended badly, and we were blown away by the response.

Daniel said, "Sure." He paused, took some time and then said, "Why not just buy the agency?"

That option was nowhere on our radar. We'd never acquired a company before, but we were open to the idea. Wow! We quickly came to a mutually beneficial agreement to acquire the business, which ultimately led to Paul and the agency's client list being added to our team.

This was a win-win, good for Daniel, great for Paul, and awesome for us. For the next ten years and beyond, we still work with several of those acquired clients, which paid for the acquisition fifty times over. Paul continues to work closely with me and my business partner to grow the agency and has assumed many of my day-to-day duties—which has helped build the Ardent team to where it is today.

Mountain Climbing

Sometimes, asking the right question at the right time is an art form. For us, what seemed like an impossibility became possible simply by asking one question.

Reaching the summit of Mount Everest is impossible for most people in the world, and hundreds die trying. But scaling Yosemite National Park's El Capitan sheer mountain face, which is 3,200 feet from the base to the summit is even crazier. Scaling it without a rope—that's insane. Even throwing a lot of money at the effort won't make it happen either. Only a lot of time in preparation and trust in the training is the only way for it to be possible.

If you haven't seen the *Free Solo* documentary about Alex Honnold and his goal to become the first free solo climber of El Capitan, I highly recommend it. I have done a little rock climbing, but I can't imagine doing what he did.

Free solo climbers have no help from ropes or protective gear. They have their shoes and chalk, plenty of experience and strength, and nerves made of steel. After countless solo climbs, they can't flippantly say, "I think I'll climb without ropes today." It is so dangerous, of all the climbers in the world, only about 1 percent even attempt it. Alex has over 1,000 free climbs himself.

With just one look at El Capitan, any experienced climber would scream, "There isn't any way to climb this. No way would I risk it without ropes." It's 3,200 feet of relentless, sheer granite, something like scaling a wall of glass.

But Alex saw the sheer rock face as an opportunity to do what no other climber had ever done. In preparation, he climbed with ropes through different scenarios, imagining how he could do it without ropes. He made notes and studied them, knowing he would not have the luxury of making even one mistake. Hold after hold, going through each step with perfect precision was an art form in itself. Mentally, he had to be prepared as this would be a very different climb. There was no way back if he climbed too far.

Knowing how and actually doing it are two different things. Alex had the physical ability. He knew how to make the climb. But doing it without ropes? That was another matter. Something was sure to go wrong. And it did.

The tension was high among his crew as he started the climb without ropes. Alex came to a point in the climb and stopped. Something wasn't right. He wasn't ready and the first attempt ended early. The correct mindset is just as important, if not more important, than the physical climb, itself—especially under stressful situations.

In business, you've probably had days like this, when you thought you were ready, only to find out that you weren't. It happens. It's normal. So don't let that deter your thinking. Your preparedness just needs more work. When fully prepared, you will be hard to stop.

Alex's crew had their doubts after the early exit. Alex did too, but he was not about to give up. He stayed focused on his goal, preparing for the next time he would try again, on that day when he would succeed.

Without the media knowing, at 5:32 a.m. on June 3, 2018, Alex began the climb that would make history. With each carefully placed foothold, his hands tightly gripping the rock, one reach after another, he inched a little higher. Then he came to the first big maneuver where he had stopped before. Everyone watching was overwhelmed, wondering if he would keep going, because after this point, there was no turning back. Quickly, like it was nothing, he made the move and kept climbing. One by one, each obstacle was tackled with precision as Alex scaled higher and higher. Less than four hours later, he achieved the unthinkable. He reached the summit. The thrill above all thrills.

As an entrepreneur, exponential thinking can seem crazy, but that is how success is achieved. Look at some of the most successful entrepreneurs in history. All were exponential thinkers—people like Elon Musk, Jeff Bezos, and Steve Jobs. They did what other said couldn't be done, but it wasn't easy. It never is.

What people do not always see is the preparation and planning that occurs for years in advance. That is what makes this story so important. Alex's preparation and planning was so detailed and thought out, he wasn't going to fail. His life was on the line. Every movement had to be precise. The weather had to be right, and physically, he had to be ready. All these keys came together at the right time to fulfill his vision and create an amazing masterpiece of success.

A Magic Vision

On the basketball court, Magic Johnson was amazing, and his vision was superb. He anticipated moves and saw openings that most players would miss. History will tell you he was one of the best point guards in the game.

But basketball wasn't his only strength. He's also proved himself as a savvy entrepreneur. Over the years, Magic Johnson Enterprises has invested in 125 Starbucks

Stores and 31 Burger King franchises. He invested in movie theaters, 24 Hour Fitness, and EquiTrust Insurance. His net worth has been estimated at $1.2 billion.

His Starbucks story stands out, not that he owned 125 locations but that he convinced the organization to trust him and build a model around the black community. Nice. You see, many businesses build a model and expect it to fit everywhere, like the proverbial square peg that we insist should fit a round hole. Nope. Doesn't work. And we shouldn't be surprised.

Starbucks felt their model would not work in black communities. Why? Simple demographics and they tried. This has nothing to do with race. It's simply recognizing unique attitudes and tastes in different communities. So Starbucks' square-peg model wasn't going to fit the communities where Magic saw a need.

On one trip to Starbucks, Magic noticed how many Latinos and African Americans would drive many miles just to have their favorite latte or coffee. He was one of them. As he waited in line, he asked questions to other guests and assessed the store as it related to the community. Hi creative mind started to see what others could not. Immediately, he knew the music would have to change. Instead of the typical jazzy style music, maybe some R&B would be a better fit in the environment. The scones weren't right. What is a scone? How about some sweet potato pie, peach cobbler, and pecan pie? *Much better*, he thought.

Magic built a successful business model by knowing who he was trying to reach. For a round hole, he needed a round peg. Many aspiring business owners agonize over how they will sell their products. Know your customer. Find out what they want. Recognize their needs and find ways to deliver. Then your loyal customers will be your brand ambassadors for life.

We'll pay $3 for a coffee, but we don't know what a scone is. — Magic Johnson[1]

Growing a business requires new ideas that come only by encouraging creative thinking. And that happens as you expand your own mindset.

Magic had the creative imagination that allowed him to see what Starbucks executives couldn't see—both the why and how stores would become successful with his model. If you want to build an exponential mindset, start with expanding your creative mind. That will help you identify and see potential that you would have missed, otherwise. You'll see what steps need to be taken, and you'll know it's worth taking the risks to make it happen.

Exercise: Let's try something. Get your notebook out and ask yourself, *What if?* What if … we could reach a million people in five years. Okay, great. Expand that mindset even more. What if … we could reach a million businesses? A million businesses could have ten million people in them. Keep expanding your mind. Think big and expand the possibilities.

After *What if?* Let's go to *And What?* What are the long-term possibilities or consequences of the what-if scenarios? Now reverse engineer the what-ifs into a future plan that could be made a reality.

---

1   https://medium.com/@grantcardone/magic-johnson-built-125-starbucks-this-is-how-he-did-it-449d18cc2f07

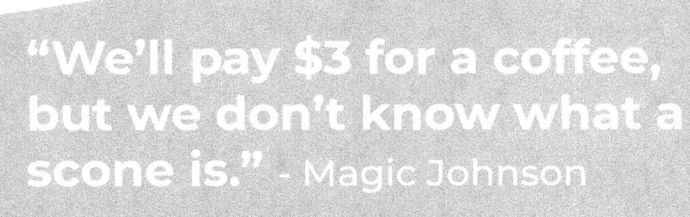

"We'll pay $3 for a coffee, but we don't know what a scone is." - Magic Johnson

Points to Ponder

- Focus on long-term, exponential growth: Think strategically about goals, processes, and outcomes. Stagnation can be dangerous, sometimes fatal. Aiming for doubling or tripling business size can unlock untapped potential.
- Learn to delegate: Entrepreneurs must abandon a do-it-yourself mindset to empowering and trusting employees to handle crucial tasks.
- Find the right people for the right roles: Only hire individuals who share the company's vision and methods. Acquiring other businesses can provide much-needed talent.

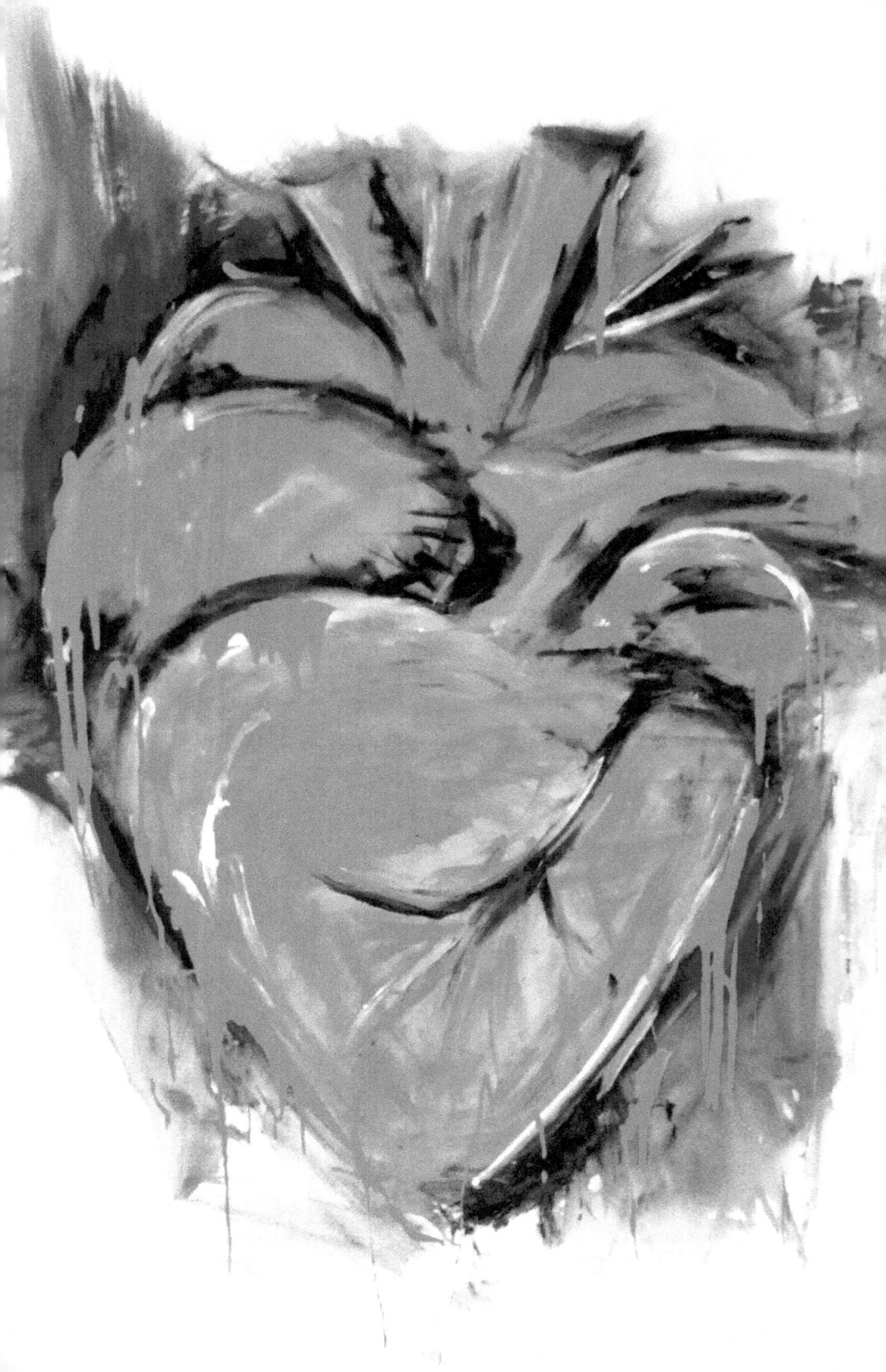

Courage to Take Risks

In the world of entrepreneurship, risks and failures aren't just normal—they're key steps on the path to real success. The most successful entrepreneurs aren't the ones who avoid risks, but they are those who learn to calculate and navigate wisely.

Four-Letter Word

Fear of failure will kill the entrepreneurial spirit. For many, *fail* is a four-letter curse word that should never be spoken in public.

I don't want to get into politics, but I think we'd love to elect legislators who were open and honest, eager to admit their mistakes and share what they've learned from their failures.

Yes, failures bring painful losses, but they're a necessary investment to achieve greatness. Our victories would be meaningless if they were easy.

Artists often welcome failure. I had to learn that mindset. The imperfections make art beautiful and make diamonds much more valuable than synthetic lab-grown gems. Even for my personal speed paintings, the rawness and originality of the work make it special. They are not perfect by any means, and they do not need to be.

Sometimes I was disappointed with my work. I stepped back, embarrassed at how poorly I had performed. Yet people loved it, proving that beauty lies in the eye of the beholder. We can often be too hard on ourselves.

Why should we be embarrassed when we fail? Did we expect it to be easy? If it were easy, then we should be embarrassed for thinking too highly of ourselves.

Trash Talk

One person's trash can be another person's treasure.

At one painting event, I had a very difficult concept to develop in just a few minutes. I was joining a national singer, so the pressure to perform well was immense. I got lost in the movement of music and added too much paint. This proved to be a big problem that I couldn't take back in the short time remaining. The piece looked like what I would call *mud*, because mixing a bunch colors produces a brown mess. Did I stop? No, I tried to take some paint off and let it dry. I kept working on it, trying to overcome the initial failure.

With such failures, I learned crucial lessons in what to do and what not to do. Trial and error can sometimes be the best teacher. Based on my experience in the world of artistry, I believe every sketch artist, painter, and designer has, at one time or another, done their best and wound up trashing the work. Artists must experiment with what doesn't work so they can know what does.

Comedians spend months working on a show by testing bits out in small venues. They learn what jokes get laughs and the ones that might as well be included in an obituary. Garrison Keillor says we don't know how to really tell a story until we've told it a dozen times. Like Alex Honnold climbed El Capitan alone without a rope, we keep practicing and failing until we're prepared and are ready and able to take the risks.

The preparation process doesn't happen overnight. Comedians work their acts night after night until the laughter builds to a rewarding crescendo. Musicians collaborate and tweak notes and lyrics until the melody and the message earns a roaring applause at the concert.

Nothing happens overnight for entrepreneurs, either. The more they prepare, build and shape their businesses, the more they minimize the risks and move toward greater success. They know change may come, but the preparation ensures, no matter what the future brings, success is on the horizon.

Calculated Gamble

Great poker players in Las Vegas are fully aware that they might lose on any given hand. In a single night, most people wind up losing whatever they've gained, but somehow the great players keep coming out on top. How? They know they might lose, but they've learned to play the odds. That is, a good bet is knowing you have a better chance of winning than losing, and the cost of losing won't take you out of the game.

Strategy and mental awareness are crucial. There are times in life when everyone has to risk something. Driving to work doesn't seem to be a gamble, but there's always a chance that another driver could do something stupid and crash into you. We call them *accidents* when we didn't see the danger. That's especially true in business.

We need strategy and mental awareness to prepare for what's coming, whether we anticipate it or not. You'll win some and lose some. Be good at measuring the odds against the potential loss, and you'll tend to come out on top.

In the movie *Rounders*, Matt Damon plays the character Mike, a law student who falls deep into the underground gambling world. Even the best poker players have great hands that lose. A whole night at the tables can go sour. The *Rounders* movie is true-to-life, full of risks and rewards along the way.

At one point in the movie, Mike is on a poker high. Even his losers were winning. Playing Texas Hold'em was returning rich rewards, but he wanted more—specifically to take down the Russian club owner, Teddy KGB. He goes all-in with the top pair on the flop and ends with a full house beneath the 9's showing. Thinking he was in the lead, he baited the club owner into betting more. The problem was that Teddy was dealt two Aces and had the better full house. Quickly Mike realized he had miscalculated. He lost the hand and $30,000. Suddenly his winnings and savings were gone. Everything was gone, and he was left in anguish.

Later, he gets redemption on Teddy, but he made one statement that I'll never forget: "Few players recall big pots they have won, strange as it seems, but every player can remember with remarkable accuracy the outstanding tough beats of his career. I can remember I bet it all on a high-stakes game in Atlantic City, and I won big. But I can't stop thinking how I lost it. Seems true to me. Cause walking in here, I can hardly remember how I built my bankroll, but I can't stop thinking of how I lost it."

Remembering Wins

How easily we can forget all the wins along the way, which got us to where we are, or we would be much worse off. Instead, we remember all the losses and imagine how perfect life would be if we hadn't made the wrong move.

Since we so clearly remember when we have failed, we do well to record our successes, because that will allow us to appreciate where we are and know that even greater day lie ahead.

Future success is best built upon past successes. We can't build upon the failures that say we're not good enough, that we'll never make it. No, we build on the success of the failure. What's that? The important lesson we learned about what *not* to do. That's the positive part we add to all our other success records. Then, we can press on with confidence.

Your vision must focus on what's ahead, not what's behind. Entrepreneurs like Jeff Bezos have proved the importance of that approach. For years, Amazon lost money. Some were sure the enterprise would fail, and now it's a resource nobody can do without, becoming one of the most valuable companies of all time.

Bezos believed in what he was doing. What others thought didn't matter. Even with the failures, he saw opportunities for success and celebrated the wins along the way.

Forward thinking will take you where you want to go. It's worth the risk.

Preparation for the future is key. Risks can be calculated and planned for success. Here are a few key points that can help in planning for what might be ahead.

- Scenario Planning: Develop multiple future scenarios and create contingency plans
- SWOT Analysis: Identify Strengths, Weaknesses, Opportunities, and Threats
- "What If?" Exercise: Imagine various possibilities and their impacts
- Trend Analysis: Study and project current market trends
- Financial Forecasting: Create detailed projections for different scenarios
- Customer Behavior Predictions: Analyze past data to predict future behaviors
- Risk Assessment: Identify potential risks and develop mitigation strategies
- Competitive Analysis: Assess competitors' strategies and market positions
- Technology Impact Assessment: Evaluate effects of emerging technologies
- Stakeholder Input: Gather insights from employees, customers, and suppliers
- Regular Review and Adjustment: Make forecasting an ongoing process

Points to Ponder

- Embrace failure as a necessary part of growth: Overcoming the fear of failure is crucial for moving forward, building resilience, and improving strategies.
- Learn by trial and error: Like artists and comedians, entrepreneurs learn by experimenting, failing, and refining ideas as they master their craft.
- Gain confidence with preparation: Apparent overnight successes are actually due to extensive planning, testing, and practice, which minimizes the risk and leads to eventual success.

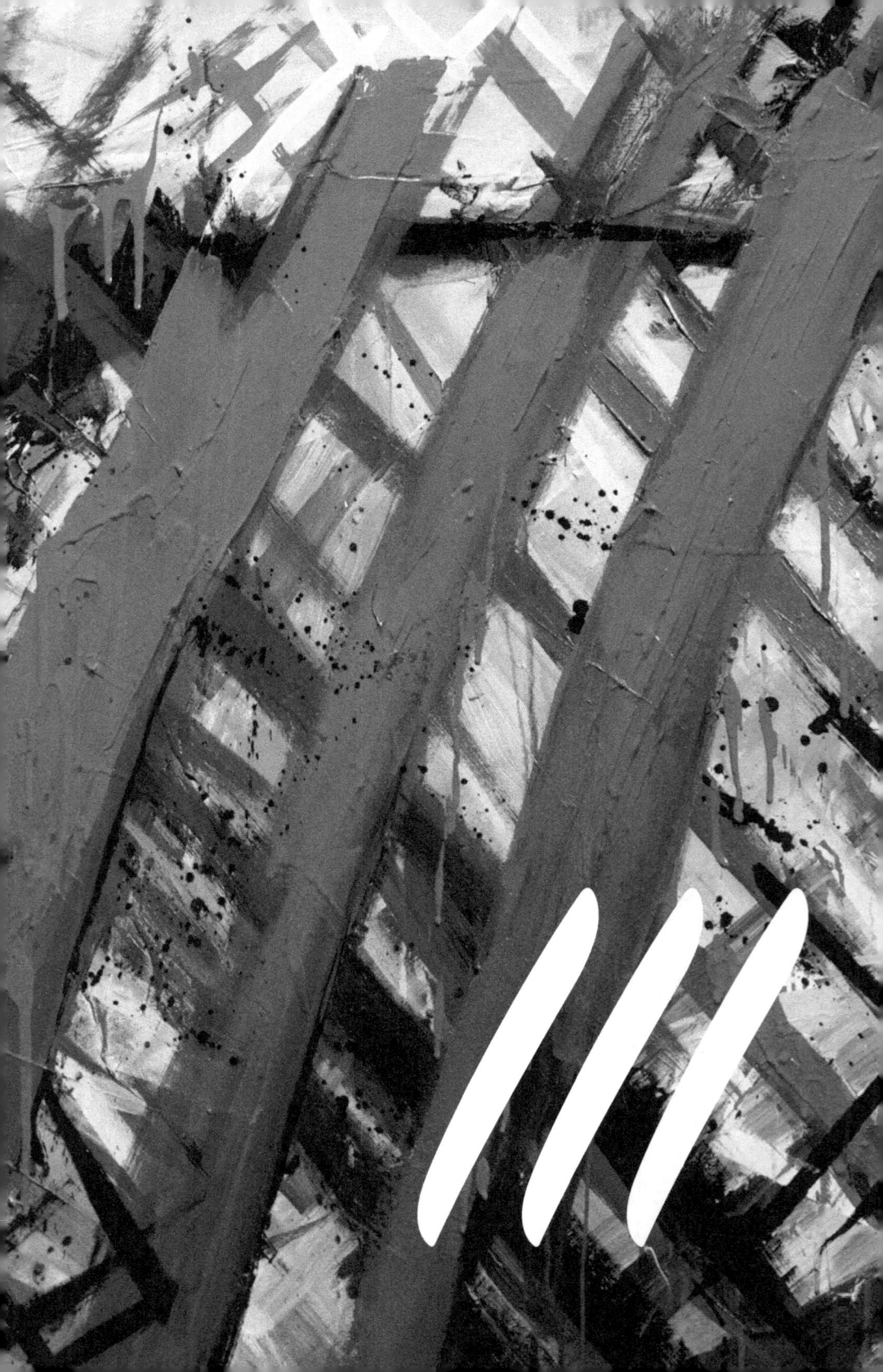

Brushstrokes
of Mastery

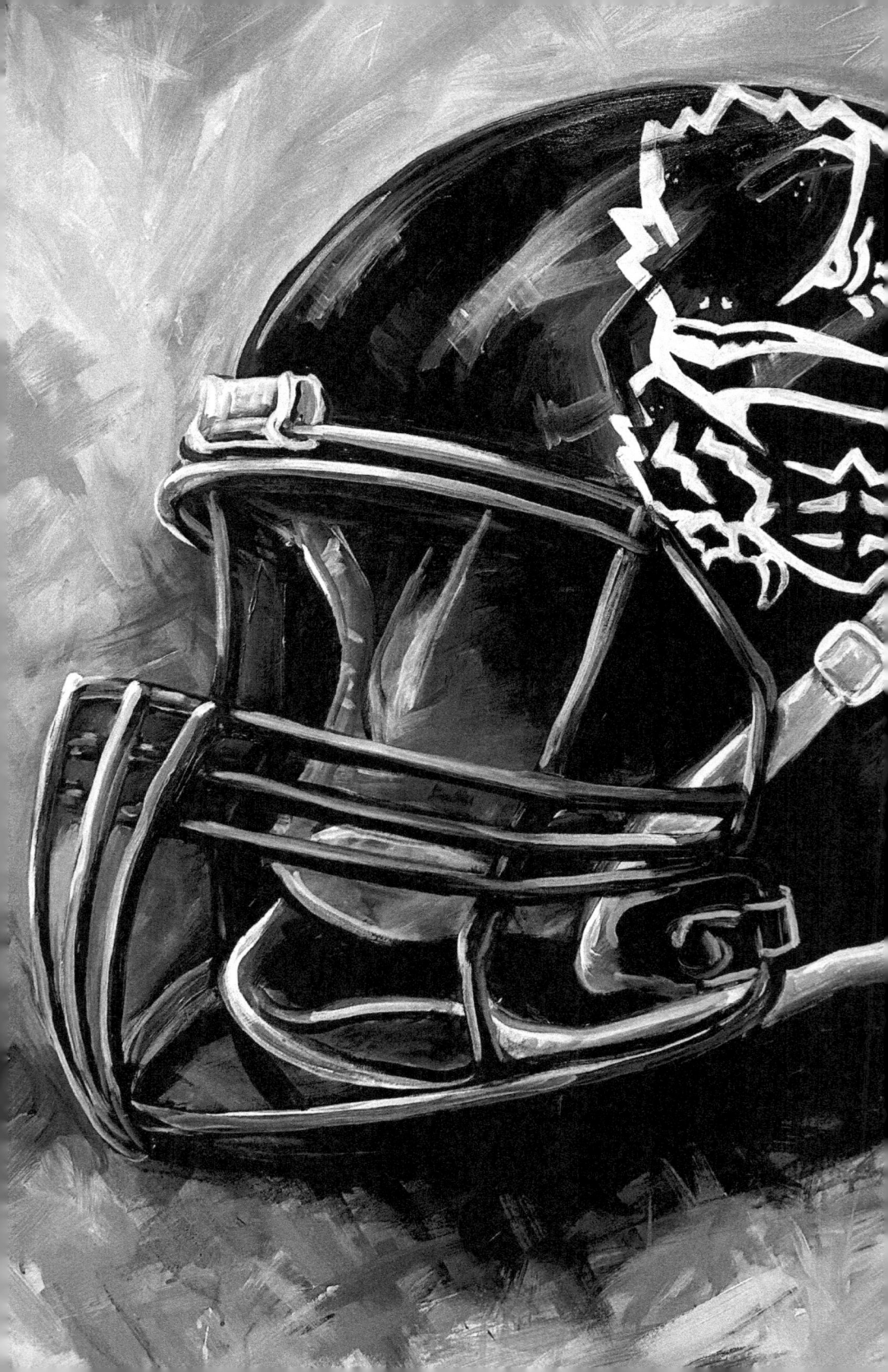

The
Art of
Stability

The entrepreneurial landscape is filled with challenges that test our resilience and adaptability—a winding road of trials and triumphs. This highlights the need to build a solid foundation for your enterprise. Like an artist preparing a canvas, entrepreneurs must lay a solid foundation to support their visions. Beyond financial stability and a strong business plan, this foundation includes a resilient company culture, adaptable strategies, and a clear, unwavering purpose to withstand market shifts, technological disruptions, and unexpected challenges.

Sculpting Strength

Even if you are not an art fan, you probably have seen Michelangelo's *David*. This beautiful marble sculpture has been an icon of the artistry world for centuries. Nothing is random about this sculpture. The pose, muscle definition, weight distribution, and balance—everything was calculated and created with perfect precision. Michelangelo's artistic genius and subsequent historic preservation has helped this work of art stand proud for everyone to see to this day.

Sculptors like Michelangelo had to incorporate specific supporting features into the sculpture to prevent collapse. One of the weakest parts in the human body is the ankle because our entire body weight is distributed upon that particular area. All the muscles and bones work together to support the strongest and weakest parts. Stone does not have the same ability, so sculptors had to plan for the extreme weight distribution. In Thomas Ridgeway Gould's *The West Wind,* for example, the figure's short and slender ankles are poised delicately upon the balls of her small feet. This would not be possible without the deliberate decision by Gould to distribute almost all of the marble's weight to her massive, flowing skirt. In *David,* Michelangelo added a tree stump around the right calf and angle. This was to enlarge and support the additional weight the ankle area had to hold. Both of these examples show how the artists reinforced the foundations to handle the weight above.

Just like a sculptor needs to make sure their creations stand on its own, entrepreneurs need to build businesses that can handle the pressure of growth and market shifts. Your business foundation isn't just about your product or service—it's about your team, your processes, your culture, and your ability to adapt. It is your job as the leader and artist to foresee the stress the business could sustain and address it. Otherwise, under too much stress, the business could fracture and even collapse.

We have seen collapses throughout the last 100 years. Companies rise and fall—names like Enron, RadioShack, Blackberry and Kodak, companies that had great starts and a foundation that appeared to be sound, only to be passed up with technology as their industries evolved.

Enron was full of corporate fraud, but RadioShack and Kodak's collapses stemmed from a series of strategic missteps and a failure to adapt to the digital revolution. Despite inventing the first digital camera in 1975, Kodak's leadership held on to their profitable film business, blinded by past successes. Resistant to change, they missed crucial opportunities to shift, made questionable strategic decisions, and were slow to respond to clear market shifts. Kodak's story isn't one of deceit like Enron, but of missed opportunities and lack of vision. As creative leaders, we must learn from Kodak's mistakes and be vigilant and open to change, or our foundations will be prone to crack and collapse.

Is the foundation of your business strong enough to sustain all that the work demands? Is it strong enough to handle significant growth? What happens when success stagnates? These questions and many others need to be asked, no matter where you are on the journey.

Learning from Others

Not every sculptor from the Renaissance had to learn the hard way—from their mistakes. No doubt, somebody led the way and sculpted the perfect marble statue only to learn that the beautiful maiden couldn't support her own weight. Make that mistake once, and you wouldn't do that again. The loss is too great.

The same can be said if we "see" someone make a mistake. Hopefully, seeing it will keep us from making the same mistakes, because we can reduce the cost of success by learning from the mistakes of others.

The Test of Time

Even to this day, some are worried that the *David* sculpture could crumble under its own weight. Years of pressure have caused microfractures in its ankles.[2] The carved tree stump at the base is also at risk. Much of the sculpture's 5.5 tons rests on its left leg and the tree stump.

After more than 300 years, *David* was replaced by a copy for public viewing. From Florence's Piazza della Signoria, the original was moved inside to La Dalleria dell'Accademia. Vibrations from millions of automobiles and tourists viewing that stature had made *David* vulnerable.

One fear some experts have is that if an earthquake hit Florence, sculptures like *David* would be destroyed. For the statue to be really safe, it needs to be earthquake proof. Obviously, an earthquake hasn't happened, but what if it did?

Then you have to ask, "Where is my business vulnerable?" When everything is going great, we can feel invincible. But that can be an illusion. I have seen it many times with clients we have worked with. At one moment things are great, but all of the sudden, there's a shaking.

At best, we can cast vision and creatively plan for our businesses, but we need earthquake-immune foundations.

---

2   https://www.staugustine.com/story/news/nation-world/2014/05/03/
michelangelos-david-danger-collapse/16118594007/

Deceptive Appearance

A tourist would look at *David* and appreciate its beauty without imagining any possibility that something could go wrong. Others with expert eyes and sophisticated instruments have worked to ensure its stability, as best they can.

As hurricanes continue to prove, buildings looking good is not the same as being good enough to withstand unanticipated storms. In our businesses, we should allow ourselves room to be concerned, even when everything is looking good.

Suppose your business has been moving along just fine. The little fractures are hardly noticeable, but the closer you look, the more you see a problem building.

Maybe you are crushing the competition so well that failure is an impossibility—until a new firm joins the fray, with something entirely different and better. Suddenly, you see how vulnerable you really are.

No matter how large or small a business is, we all have to deal with problems we never anticipated. Every business is broken somewhere, and if the issues are not addressed properly, the long-term effects can be catastrophic.

As an entrepreneur, you have to see the sculpture of your business as something of beauty, but don't let yourself become too enraptured with your success.

Upon Closer Inspection

Let's think about your work now. Where are the issues or cracks? Maybe all the weight is on the top. Are you the only one supporting that weight? Is there another point of stress within the business that needs to be addressed? Now is the time to ask such questions. Otherwise, outside forces may do it for you—when it's too late.

We have dealt with this within our agency on several occasions. The biggest issues stemmed from rapid growth. During our first eight years, my partner and I handled sales, account management, design, and websites. But then it was too much for us to handle.

For the business to grow, we needed to delegate most of what we were doing so we could focus on what we had no time to do. We had to develop team leads, build a sales team, and appoint account managers. Mistakes were going to happen, and we made many.

Bottled Up in Bottlenecks

Like it or not, experience is the best teacher. We may read books, attend seminars, and seek professional advice, but ultimately, the application of what we know is the means to determine what will or won't work for us. The sooner we can put an improvement to the test, the better.

We think we know. But the truth is, we don't know what we don't know. That condition is unavoidable. The doing is our educator, pass or fail. And yes, failure is essential, or we're not caring and trying hard enough.

One of our biggest failures was not understanding the difference between *project* management and *account* management. Since we were small, we hired one person for both jobs. We soon learned that one personality doesn't split effectively for the distinctly different needs. Neither aspect of the work was being done well.

The two roles required completely different personalities, but we compounded the error by having everything funnel through one person, creating a major bottleneck. One person handling 100 percent of projects and communication quickly became a severe problem, with issues that had to be addressed.

- Missed tasks and deadlines
- Errors and mistakes
- Burnout
- Breakdown in communication
- Misallocation of resources
- Client expectations management

Thankfully, I quickly saw the problem and adjusted to alleviate the bottleneck. This meant hiring and allocating resources across a few team members. Now, instead of a bottleneck, we have a process around a team focused on specific deliverables with their own roles.

With a natural workflow, our bottleneck was removed, and the business expanded. Changing work demands can create unexpected bottlenecks and hinder growth, so watch for them and find solutions as soon as possible.

Project and Account Managers

Our project managers needed to love details more than a strawberry sundae. While planning timelines and working out schedules, they had to be sure every *i* was dotted and every *t* was crossed. The more detail, the more they thrived, which meant they had little time to deal with customers.

Account managers had the opposite concern, making care for the client much more important than the minute details. They were the company's "face," taking projects from the initial sales team and then building the relationship with the client. Their *Job One* was to ensure that the company delivered what the client wanted. This was done by working closely with project managers to be sure estimates and timelines were accurate. They built relationships with the client, and this connection enabled upsells of additional services.

Account managers are powerful sales tools that continue to build the foundation of our business for thousands of clients, from startups to Fortune 100 companies, many from the early days that are still clients today.

Owner's Pet Project

Owners can have a hard time handing off a favorite client to be served by someone else. I am guilty as charged.

When we hired Paul, we knew he was a TCU grad, which gave him a personal interest in the brand. For years, I had worked with almost every school and department within the university, but as the university hired more in-house personnel, they did not need our services as often.

I understood the situation but made sure our communication channels remained open. This meant delegating much of the relationship to alums on our team and their account manager.

At the close of the 2022 football season, the TCU Marketing and Communication team reached out to us about helping them with the playoffs and potential national championship advertising.

Even though I had worked with TCU for over twenty years, the team took this project on from start to finish, with the account manager taking the lead, *not me*.

The account manager worked with the creative director and project manager to quote, strategize, and plan the work to implement a campaign for TCU. This advertising included airport digital signage, hotel signage, program ads, newspaper ads, and billboards.

This was all done with very little input from me. Honestly, I was proud that they didn't need me. The team handled everything in collaboration with TCU.

The result was remarkable, garnering national attention. Seeing social media abuzz and news media sharing our work was a thrill. Tweets like, "Just landed at the Phoenix airport and TCU is running 'Horned Frogs thrive in the desert' ads. SO BADASS." — Barstool TCU.

In Retrospect

Upon completion of the TCU campaign, I was delighted because I saw firsthand how important it was for each person on the team to be focused on their individual responsibilities.

The project didn't focus on one person, but a team who worked together through its completion. This included as many as five people in different roles from copywriting and art direction to account management. Each role played a vital part in the campaign's success.

What had once been a bottleneck had now become a strength because of proper positioning of each individual.

Time for Appraisal

Take a few minutes to creatively consider your situation. Slow down enough to reflect on your greatest strengths and assets. What is the foundation of those assets? Are they well-placed and secure?

What are your greatest weaknesses? What steps might be needed to compensate for weaknesses and build upon your strengths? If the cracks and micro fractures aren't addressed, they won't get better. They are sure to worsen over time. So there's no better time than now to fix them.

If there are cracks in your foundation, the superstructure won't stand a larger superstructure. They must be repaired.

Your creative genius lies in taking time to look at your situation from top to bottom, assessing the pieces along the way. As you repair the foundation, you will see how all the pieces stack upon one another so your foundation can support your organization's weight.

Foundation Checklist:

Financial Health

- ☐ Track sales revenue.
- ☐ Monitor net profit and profit margins.
- ☐ Analyze cash flow.
- ☐ Keep an eye on operating expenses.

Customer Metrics

- ☐ Measure customer acquisition costs.
- ☐ Calculate customer lifetime value.
- ☐ Track customer satisfaction rates.
- ☐ Monitor customer retention/churn rate.

Operational Efficiency

- ☐ Evaluate productivity metrics.
- ☐ Assess quality control measures.
- ☐ Monitor inventory turnover.
- ☐ Track on-time delivery rates.

Marketing and Sales

- ☐ Measure conversion rates.
- ☐ Track lead generation.
- ☐ Analyze customer engagement metrics.
- ☐ Monitor return on marketing investment.

Employee Performance

- ☐ Track employee productivity.
- ☐ Measure employee satisfaction.
- ☐ Monitor turnover rates.
- ☐ Assess training and development progress.

Strategic Planning

- ☐ Define clear business objectives and goals.
- ☐ Regularly review and update your business plan.
- ☐ Conduct SWOT analyses.
- ☐ Monitor industry trends & competitive landscape.

Innovation and Growth

- ☐ Track new product/service development.
- ☐ Measure research and development investments.
- ☐ Monitor market share growth.
- ☐ Assess expansion into new markets or segments.

Risk Management

- ☐ Identify and monitor potential risks.
- ☐ Implement and track compliance measures.
- ☐ Assess cybersecurity measures.
- ☐ Monitor supplier relationships and diversification.

Brand and Reputation

- ◻ Track brand awareness metrics.
- ◻ Monitor online reviews and ratings.
- ◻ Measure social media engagement.
- ◻ Assess corporate social responsibility initiatives.

Technology and Infrastructure

- ◻ Evaluate IT system efficiency.
- ◻ Track technology adoption rates.
- ◻ Monitor data security measures.
- ◻ Assess scalability of business systems.

What forces could have the greatest impact the strengths (positive or negative)? Assess each point, identify, and plan accordingly.

Points to Ponder

- Regularly assess the business's structural integrity: Learn from the mistakes of corporate giants that have fallen and look for unseen problems like bottlenecks or poor management that could cause long-term damage.
- Delegate tasks and responsibilities: As a business rapidly expands, leaders must acquire or train employees to handle the increased workload. Splitting roles between detail-oriented project managers and client-focused account managers can prevent bottlenecks and improve efficiency.
- Prepare for unanticipated risks: Entrepreneurs must assess hidden vulnerabilities from market shifts and economic downturns.

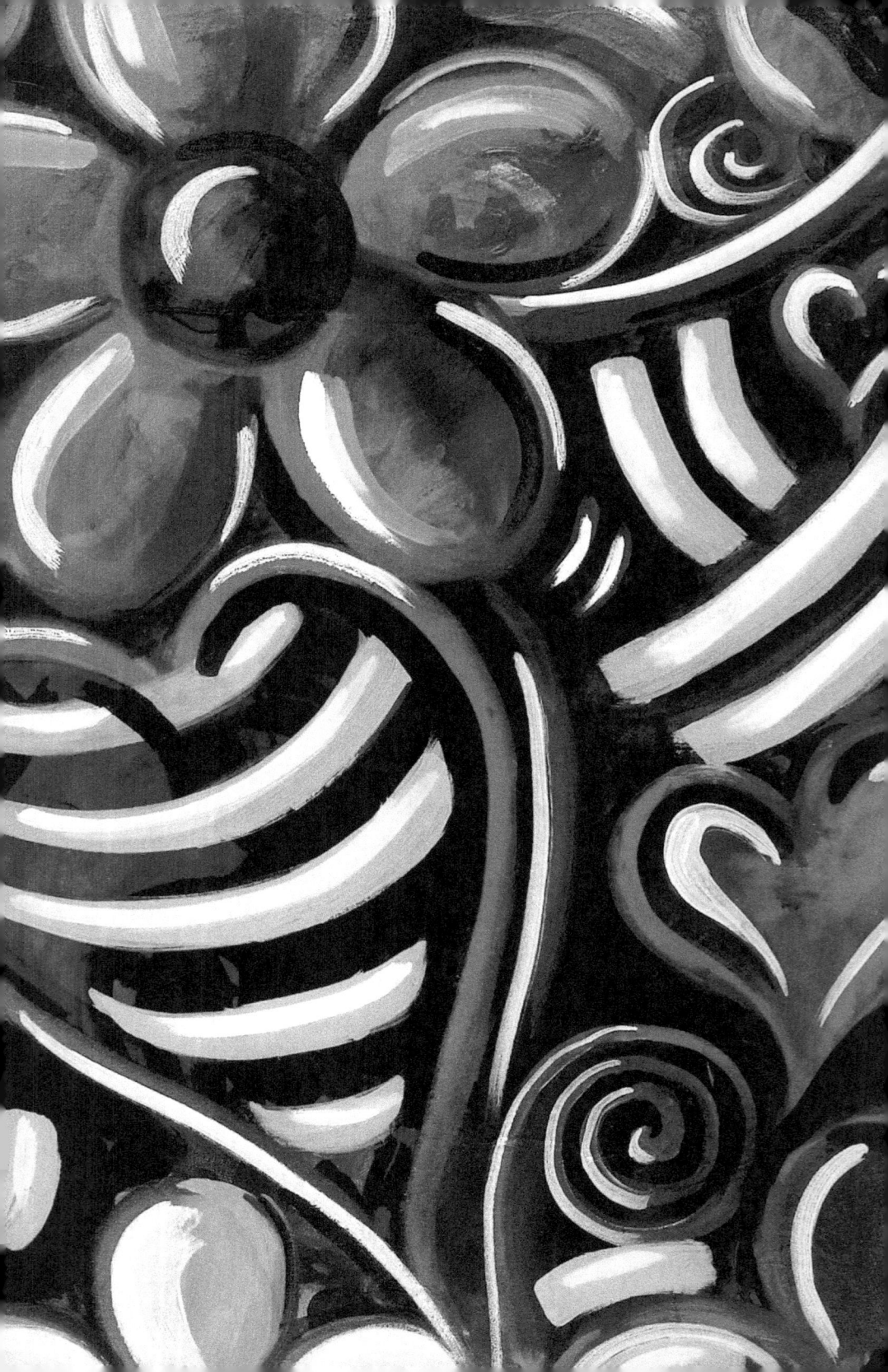

The Art of Strategy

Strategic planning is one of the most artistic, creative, and important parts of business. The best ideas can fail for a variety of reasons, but without a decent strategy, success is no more than an accident.

Age of Technology

These days, our minds spend a lot of time on electronic devices without the need for physical strategies involving chess, checkers, or Monopoly. Depending on how you use the technology, this can be either good or bad. In an endless pit of screen swipes, time becomes a blur, often with very little accomplished.

In my college years, I played all kinds of games with friends. *Halo* was one of my favorites. Video games were fun, but the old board games involved more strategy and not so much hand-eye coordination. One game that we played the most was called *Risk*.

Winning at Risk

I soon learned to not take stupid risks, but calculated risks were an important part of the game that revolved around the idea of world domination. The board is a colorized world map divided into territories across Earth's continents. To win, I had to be patient and forward-thinking to conquer the world.

Each player has a series of cards naming a territory for placing armies. On my turn, I might reinforce my territory by adding armies, then launch an attack on my opponent's adjacent territory, the moves determined by dice rolls. If I successfully conquered a territory, I gained a card to exchange for more armies.

The game ends when one player conquers the entire world map, eliminating all other players. I had to strategize when to attack, defend, or forge alliances. Winning combines elements of strategy, negotiation, and some luck—much like some of the challenges we face in business, making it a dynamic and engaging experience each time I played.

One game required four to eight hours of methodical anticipating, planning, and strategizing until one of us conquered the world. Each month, we gathered to play. Any newcomer never had a chance. Developing a winning strategy required a lot of experience from losing.

In the beginning, I started strong because I loved strategy board games and came with a decent amount of experience, but I still had a lot to learn. My creative mindset and ability to anticipate moves helped a lot. But I was also bold and impatient, which led to my defeat time after time, until I learned to adjust to each situation and find the best strategy.

Patience for the Prepared Mind

Seize control of Australia. That was my primary objective because there was only one way to invade the continent, making it the easiest to defend. With each turn with control of Australia, I received a bonus of two armies.

With Australia secured, the game became a test of patience and flexible strategy based on what other players did. Every round, I wanted to attack at least one territory and earn a card while steadily reinforcing my own territories. While strengthening my positions with each turn, I watched my opponents battle among themselves and waited for the right moment to pick them off, one by one.

Patience. The game demanded it, and that was good practice for me. And then the strategy, making calculated decisions about when to move and when to wait.

Sounds a lot like the business world, doesn't it?

Seizing Opportunities

Like the game of *Risk*, business strategies must incorporate a delicate balance between risk-taking and caution, knowing when to attack and when to bide your time. We must know when to be aggressive and when to back off, be patient, and make the right move at the appropriate time.

When Dollar Shave Club launched in 2011, they saw an opportunity to shake up an industry dominated by big names. Companies like Gillette had a chokehold on the market, with huge budgets and control of the retail shelves. But instead of being intimidated, Dollar Shave Club took a bold, calculated risk. They went straight for the jugular with a subscription-based model that offered affordable razors delivered right to your door.

Their launch strategy was pure creative genius. A funny, low-budget YouTube ad went viral, putting them on the map almost overnight. It was a risky move, similar to the board game Risk, where one bold attack could either lead to a big win or a huge loss. Their gamble worked, and suddenly they were in the spotlight.

What made the strategy so risky wasn't just their approach to selling razors. They disrupted the whole business model. Instead of following the traditional retail route, they went direct-to-consumer with a subscription service. At the time, other products tried and failed, but they believed in the strategy, and it worked.

Within just a few years, Dollar Shave Club built a loyal customer base and was rapidly growing. Their fresh branding, affordable pricing, and focus on customer experience helped them thrive. In 2016, they sold to Unilever for $1 billion.

Just as in Risk, where taking an unconventional path and exposing a vulnerability can lead to victory, Dollar Shave Club challenged the norm. They took bold risks, completely shaking up the market, and achieved phenomenal success. They didn't just compete with the big players. They changed the game entirely.

The ability to access your creative mind to manage risk effectively is key to success on all continents. Throughout history, artists have aimed to change the status quo. As entrepreneurs, the more we consider new ideas and new aways to approach the game, the more likely we can overcome any challenge and achieve massive success.

Strength of Alliances

Risk players often form alliances to achieve their goals, but those relationships can be fragile, temporary, and subject to betrayal. Similarly in the business world, partnerships and collaborations can be highly beneficial, but they come with their own set of risks. The stakes are much higher than walking away from a board game and flippantly saying, "Oh well, I lost."

It was many years ago, but I remember the day like yesterday. My friend David came to me after 9/11 and said, "I want to do what you do." At the time, he sold cars and wanted to get out of that game.

I coached him in what to do and how to start. A year later, he quit his job to work for himself, and I helped him expand his client base. Selling was never hard for him, but managing day-to-day operations like billing was a chore. At the time, I was focus on design and web development. He was focused on web and video.

At a lunch, we asked, "What if we joined together?" We had been passing projects back and forth based upon our expertise. It was an interesting idea, but I had to weigh the risks and rewards. I had been in business longer and made more money. What would it cost? Could we work well together? Would it damage our friendship? If we combined, we could hire someone.

Business leaders must carefully evaluate the risks and rewards associated with alliances, considering factors like trustworthiness, shared goals, and the potential for long-term success.

No doubt, you've heard that Rome wasn't built in a day. It wasn't reduced to rubble in a day, either. A board game might be won or lost in four hours, but business is a game of many years, which says the stakes are high and we need to plan ahead.

We knew the stakes were high, but we could be much stronger together. Yes, it was a risk but one worth taking. Our decision to team up in 2005 led to a long-term relationship, and we've been working together ever since. It turned out, I was great at the things David wasn't and he was great at covering my weaknesses Which meant we complemented each other very well. But most importantly, our values and perspectives were aligned. This meant as we looked toward the future, we could clearly see the path we wanted to follow.

Players must not only consider the current position but also realistically anticipate the steps needed for future expansion and dominance. Successful leaders develop and execute strategic plans that extend beyond short-term gains to focus on sustainable growth and market leadership.

Strategic Flexibility

Playing *Risk* taught me the importance of adaptability, to make adjustments in recognition of other players' maneuvering. Flexible thinking is crucial for staying competitive and thriving in our ever-changing business environment.

> ## Strategy is an art that is vital to entrepreneurial success.

By mastering these principles, business leaders can navigate the complex landscape of competition, uncertainty, and opportunity to achieve success in their endeavors.

Strategy is an art that is vital to entrepreneurial success.

Strategic Frameworks Worth Consideration

Business Model Canvas:

This is a widely used startup strategy framework for outlining the fundamental elements of a company's offering. It provides a visual template to describe a business model's key components, including value proposition, customer segments, revenue streams, and key activities. This can be very helpful when planning a new business or considering new strategic moves.

Lean Startup Framework:

Developed by Eric Ries, this framework emphasizes rapid iteration and customer feedback. It's particularly useful for startups and new business initiatives, focusing on creating a minimum viable product (MVP) and learning from customer interactions to refine the business model.

Jobs to Be Done (JTBD) Framework:

Developed by Clayton Christensen, this framework helps validate a consumer's need for a product. It's useful when starting a new business or considering new product offerings, as it focuses on understanding what "job" customers are trying to accomplish with a product or service.

Blue Ocean Strategy:

This framework encourages businesses to create new market space (blue oceans) rather than compete in existing markets (red oceans). It can be particularly useful when considering innovative new business moves or starting a business in a crowded market.

SWOT Analysis:

While not specific to new businesses, a SWOT analysis (Strengths, Weaknesses, Opportunities, Threats) can be very helpful in assessing the viability of a new business idea or strategic move.

Scenario Planning:

This involves creating and brainstorming around possible future scenarios. It can be particularly useful when starting a business in an uncertain or rapidly changing environment.

Points to Ponder

- Wait for the right moment to act: Both in games like Risk and in business, patience and timing is important to seize key opportunities.
- Employ a well-crafted strategy: Analyze business models like Canvas, Lean Startup, and Blue Ocean to tailor your best approach for creating and executing a plan for success.
- Learn from losses: Failure is an essential part of learning how to develop effective strategies.

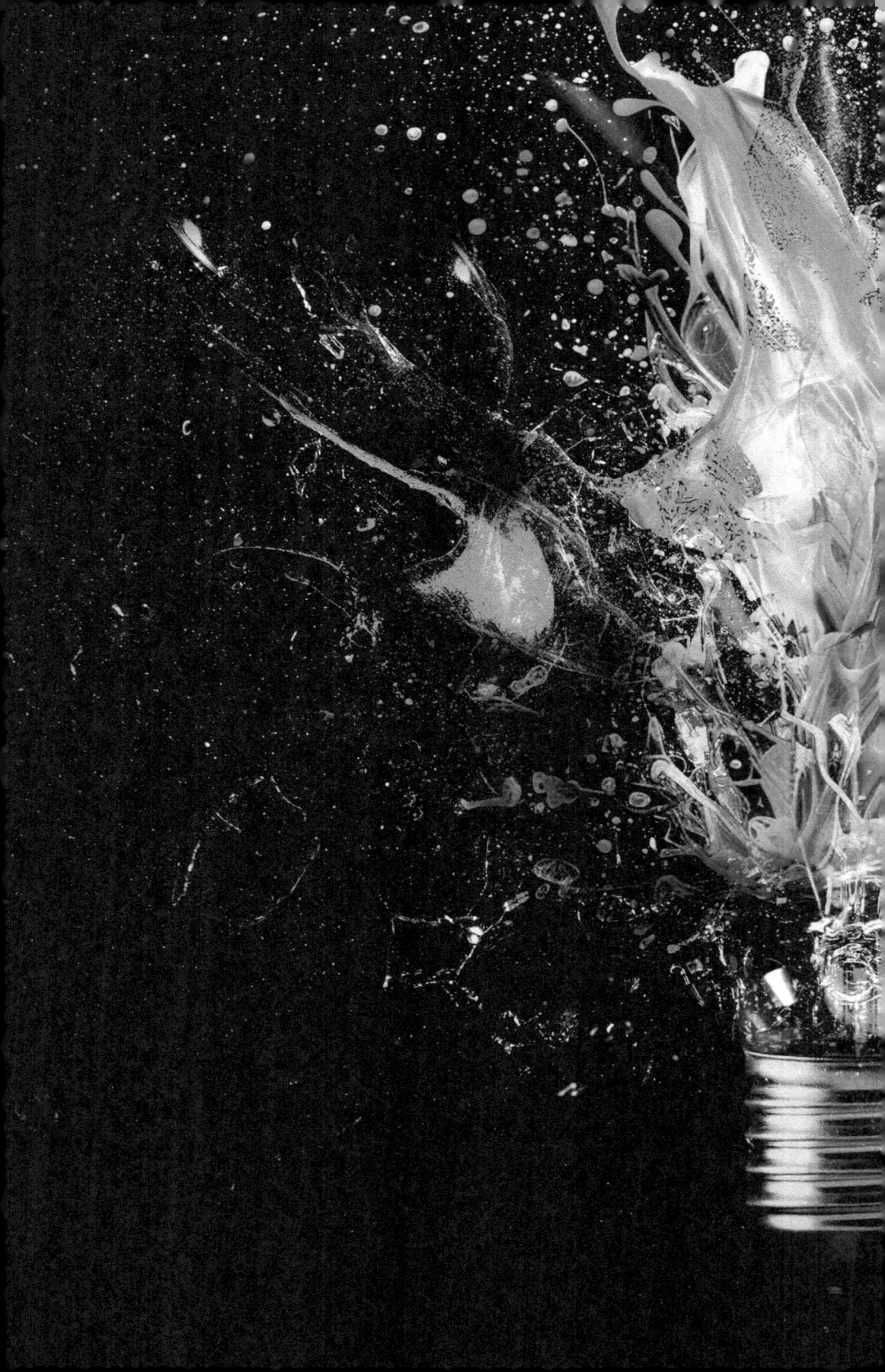

The
Art of
AI

Artificial Intelligence, or AI, refers to computer systems able to perform tasks that typically require human intelligence. For entrepreneurs, AI isn't just a buzzword—it's a powerful tool that can revolutionize how we approach business problems and innovate solutions.

In case you're curious, AI did not write this chapter. Today, more and written content, still images, and videos is being produced through AI. The technology is rapidly evolving, with some newscasts warning us that our lives will soon be replaced by machines. I don't consider myself an expert, and who really is, right now? The experts are the ones creating the AI engines. We are simply AI users. Maybe I am an expert user, but the reality is, much like any other tool, it can be wonderful when used properly but dangerous when it's not.

The Evolution of AI

If there's anything we should know about business, it's that times are always changing. The ripple effect says the pond can't remain calm when somebody drops a big rock onto the surface. When one area changes, the surrounding area will respond accordingly.

Supercomputers have advanced beyond what most people could have imagined a few years ago. There are limits, but we're still discovering what they are. AI learning started slowly but is now seeing exponential growth.

With its highspeed connection to the world wide web, we ask the computer a question and get an immediate, comprehensive response. If we want to know more, we ask more questions and get more answers. For one thing, this makes a superb learning tool for us, saving countless hours of library research and evaluation.

As more users give information to the AI, the more it learns and the more it can help us learn. What happens when people stop "feeding" it information? Without fuel, the fire can't burn, and without a supply stream of new information, AI can't learn.

Yes, AI's capabilities are rapidly evolving, but it's important to recognize that our creativity, emotional intelligence, and nuanced reasoning can never be replaced. Imagination, intuition, and contextual awareness sets us apart. The challenge lies not in AI replacing us, but rather in how it should reshape our roles and responsibilities. Those who learn to harness AI effectively—using it to augment their skills, streamline processes, and free up time for higher-level thinking—will have a significant advantage over the complacent. The risk is being outpaced by colleagues and competitors who master the art of collaboration with AI. To stay relevant, we must evolve alongside AI, using it as a powerful tool to enhance our creativity and problem-solving abilities.

One of the most decorated copywriters and marketers is Ken Moskowitz, who founded Ad Zombies. His client list includes Chevrolet, Frito-Lay, Coca-Cola, and Tampax—companies that most creatives only dream about working with. His ads have been adorned on billboards and even the Super Bowl, not once, but eight and counting. He could've had the mindset of most traditional advertisers and been resistant to change. But no, he jumped in with both feet and it revolutionized his creative.

His creative work is meant to emotionally connect to the viewer. This is something AI cannot do. *Feel*. But it can help him in the ideation process, which is best illustrated in his story behind Ooni Pizza ovens. Ooni is a home pizza oven that can cook pizzas in sixty seconds as if it came from a restaurant. He had to come up with a headline for a new ad campaign, and he wanted it to be something that would grab the attention of the viewer. So, he started asking ChatGPT a series of questions. The responses were typical but not what we were looking for. He kept pressing but gave up. AI just couldn't produce the unique feeling he was wanting. Then he asked ChatGPT how an Ooni compared to other ovens. He soon learned most ovens cook up to 450 degrees. An Ooni, 950 degrees. Boom! There was the angle and the differentiator. He pressed for more, but AI could not produce a headline that worked, but his own idea clicked. "Everything else is just half-baked." Absolute genius!

While AI couldn't produce the exact copy Ken was looking for, it was instrumental in the creative process. Could Ken had come up this without the use of AI? Eventually, perhaps. But his experience shows the benefit of including AI ideation to your processes.

The high-level creatives like Ken, the thinkers, the visionaries, and the developers who guide improvement in today's business world are irreplaceable. We're safe in our jobs for as long as we continue to advance and adjust to the use of AI tools as they evolve.

AI as an Innovative Tool

This technology is very powerful. Make no mistake about that. Do you want a good letter? A great blog? A comprehensive business plan? Just tell AI what you want, and you'll get a response in seconds. But don't think for a second that this will ever be enough.

You must still check to be sure everything is right—correcting mistakes, cutting what's irrelevant, adding what's missing, and being sure your message is exactly what you want to say. That is, the words must be from your mouth, organized and phrased like what otherwise would have taken you hours to rewrite and edit to perfection.

With the advent of computers, we heard the phrase "garbage in, garbage out." With AI, that could never be more true. So now we have AI to help us with better prompts so we can ask the best questions to get closer to the results we want.

You already know how your creativity, imagination, and innovation have been crucial to your success. Now magnify that need by an exponential factor of ten. That is, one great idea can return ten possibilities, and each of those can produce ten more—ten times ten times ten … The more imagination you have, the more you can develop the AI to create some amazing results.

AI as a Strategy Tool

Before AI can help, you must understand your goal. What do you want to accomplish? At the start, you must have a clear vision of where you want to be.

The strategy behind creating an image versus a blog post are vastly different. With minimal input, AI is very good at spitting out content, but the quality may stink enough to embarrass a skunk. Okay … maybe not that bad … but not the best, either. And you do want the best, or your AI-using competitors will pass you by.

Every question a human can think of needs to feed into the AI dataset. This might include target audience, goal, tone, length, location, and business size. The possibilities are endless, similar to a full creative brief or project brief. Some AI prompts can be several pages in length. Do you get that? If you thought AI could do all the work, you're wrong. It won't do your thinking for you.

ChatGPT, Claude, and Midjourney have been in the forefront for a long time, but there are other racecars on the track, and they aren't slowing down for a caution flag. Apple, Adobe, Gemini, and Facebook are catching up with the early players. Even photo libraries like Getty Images are jumping into AI creation. Every week, we're seeing more drivers entering the race. The AI game will be similar to a Mario Cart race. One will take the lead, a turtle will get thrown and hit the leader from behind, causing them to spin out and lose the lead. Back and forth they race to a never-ending finish line.

The finish line will always move but we have already seen the impact upon copywriters and virtual assistants. High-level copywriters can do the work of five people by building out their own dataset within ChatGPT. With AI automation, the need for video production, translation services, and voice actors won't be as great. But more will be needed in other areas, and those services will have greater value because of AI.

For a while, our lead copywriter struggled with the idea of AI. The copy was mediocre and didn't tell the story in a way a human would. Mistakes had to be fixed, and all the editing caused them to ask, "What's the point?" Well, think of AI as a junior level copywriter who could tell some of the story but didn't see the big picture. She always had to edit and rewrite for the content to be deliverable to the client. So I asked, "What's the difference?" It clicked!

Employees have only so much time to produce great work. The nature of a writer's work makes it difficult to sustain a high level of creativity for eight hours a day, every day. For her, AI served as a junior level copywriter to get down the base that could be transformed into a powerful marketing piece. As she develops her voice in the AI, the base can end up being better than any junior copywriter would typically produce. This is the power behind AI and turning a process into an art form.

Business Need for Automation

This is huge. More automation means fewer people needed to perform a task, which potentially means better margins and room for scalability. It also means you can get to market quicker.

Online chatbots can boost communication and filter leads for the best opportunities for your sales staff. With the proper script and scenarios, an AI bot can filter and engage new customers without you having to take the call. Once the conversation is ready to close or goes beyond the AI, the connection can then push out to the sales team. This allows your team to focus on high-value targets without wasting time with useless inquiries.

There are some pitfalls, because the AI conversation needs to be well thought-out and developed as if a real person is speaking. Otherwise, it will come across as fake and lead to a lack of trust in what the customer is getting.

One great example comes from my friend Roland Frasier—attorney by education, entrepreneur by action, and AI expert in secret. If anyone could turn lead into gold, I would bet on him. The man is a genius in so many ways. Not many people can pitch an idea like buying a business with no money down and then deliver. He does, and there are countless stories of people in his Epic program who have done just that.

At a conference, his extensive presentation showed how AI was being utilized in his businesses, with nugget after nugget of genius. *Air AI* can have ten- to forty-minute-long phone calls that sound like a *real* human. I knew about Air already, because my partner had a call with their sales team about utilizing the tool. I was glued to his presentation. While he talked about Air and what it could do, what really struck me was the robust backend system to automate the whole process. Most people do not realize that deep systems must be developed behind AI tools for them to be successful, especially when you are automating these tools. I can't begin to go into his whole process, but think about starting with your call list on a spreadsheet. Then put the what-if statements on a script. Outline every possible scenario for the AI to be able to communicate to the user. Then, based upon the responses, guide the user into the final sale, mostly done without the user ever talking to a human. My mind was blown at the detail and depth of the process, one that didn't come with a prompt telling AI what to do, but one that took months to build out.

The scalability of AI is immense, and by integrating AI-driven systems, you can achieve EPIC profitability. — Roland Frasier

AI as a Development Tool

All computer applications are not created equal. As AI becomes better at writing code and recognizing potential structural flaws, programmers who use AI as a programming tool will become even more valuable to handle everything that automation misses. Just like copywriting, one coder will accomplish more in less time. AI will not always get everything right, and a coder can wind up having to re-code what's needed.

We're seeing more and more AI in website development, making simple tasks even simpler, so even a child could do it. Through a series of steps or prompts, amazing sites can be created in a matter of minutes. Seriously, my friend Rachel Miller built PageWheel as a tool that can produce landing pages and content for your product—all through a few clicks and in a matter of minutes. At the same time, when unique business needs require something different and can't be automated, the development skills needed will become even more valuable.

AI tools like Relume can create wireframes and mood boards in a matter of seconds. I can prompt a fifteen-page website for a chiropractor and immediately have fifteen wires set up with headings and base content. Then with a click of a button, I can convert those wires into mood boards that can be moved, reorganized, and updated. The problem is, there is no easy way to take some of these outputs and convert them into a fully functioning website. There are tools that say they can do it, but only so well, and not to our standards.

Will AI continue to improve in this area? Absolutely. And developers will be improving their skills as well. We'll always need people who understand the code, are aware of the goal, and know what AI can and cannot deliver. AI won't help the general public complete custom projects without any understanding of code.

The expert human touch will always be needed.

AI as a Brand or Creative Tool

Branding is much more than your logo and unique colors. It is more than just your copy or company history. It is who you are, what you do, your mission, your vision, your core values, and your culture—the whole company package. Lastly, your brand is the people within your organization and the people who love the company.

AI cannot replace the brand. But … it can enhance our ability to define or outline the brand in a more streamlined process.

As a creative and branding tool, AI will become irreplaceable, especially for concepts and storyboarding. Instead of countless hours of sketching ideas and mapping out illustrations for a client presentation, we can now prompt AI to give you sample images with ease.

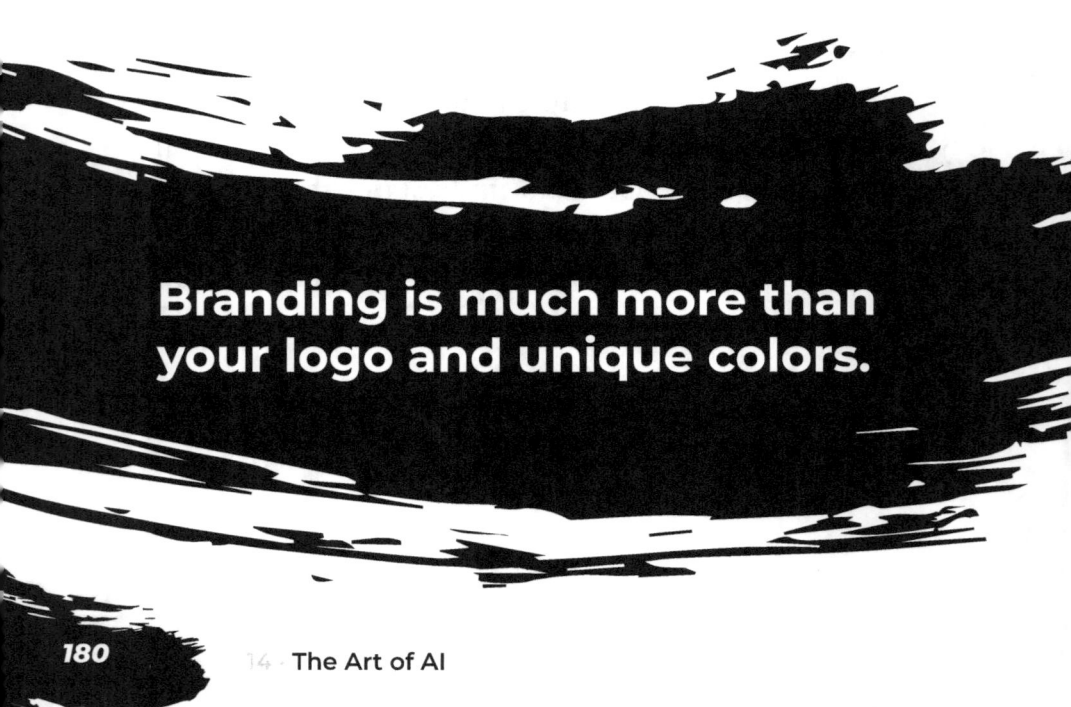

Branding is much more than your logo and unique colors.

For example, we were strategizing a photo and video shoot for a western-style high-end furniture store—something reflective of the show *Yellowstone*. In the past, picturing a nice couch in the middle of a field with longhorn cattle was something we could only describe with words or sketches. Now with AI, we can illustrate the image we are looking to create. We can present a series of those images as a storyboard for client approval and then use those images for the photographer. To communicate vision and story behind a visual campaign, the ability to ideate quickly is a game changer.

AI for branding is a little more complicated, mainly because of indefinite legal issues. Right now, we cannot copyright or trademark AI-created content, including images and logos. Why would we ever want to create a logo with AI if it can't be trademarked? We wouldn't. But just like for photography, we can use it to generate ideas that will help us create better original graphics that can be trademarked.

In writing a book about Art, there was no way I was going to use AI to create my book cover. So as I went through my creative process I started to ideate. What image would represent art, imagination, creativity, and entrepreneurs? My mind raced and then the idea hit like a light bulb going off. Literally! That was it. A lightbulb. But not just a plain lightbulb. No, this one needed to be a lightbulb exploding with various colors of paint going in all different directions. For fun, I tested Dall-e and Midjourney. Both failed miserably—nothing close to what I wanted. Midjourney did okay for the explosion of paint but not the representation of the bulb. So then I took the traditional designer route. I searched our library in Getty Images. In a matter of seconds, I found a lightbulb exploding across the page. Perfect!

Then I searched for paint splatter or explosions. I found another image, Quickly I downloaded them and went to work. I set my canvas size in Photoshop and layered each photo. It was coming together, but I wanted more color. Getty didn't have an image exactly as I wanted but Midjourney did. I grabbed the image and began to blend the images together, editing splatters, enhancing the glass, and moving pieces to just the right place to create an epic book cover.

A photoshoot would have been great, but that would've been costly and we might not have gotten just the right shot. Combining multiple images and using AI allowed my creative abilities to take over without any hindrances. This is the power of art and AI.

As we move forward, it will be hard to distinguish AI from traditional creative. The only way to distinguish creativity from AI is to utilize our humanity and imperfections. It is in these imperfections that true creators will shine in the upcoming AI revolution.

In the music world, artists can write lyrics and orchestrations in mere minutes. Some of it is pretty good, but music professionals can tell the difference. Great music still requires the human touch, or it's not good enough. Ballads of loss, heartbreaks, or joys of a newfound love require mood and feeling that AI cannot effectively create.

Daniel McCarthy, founder of three companies—MusicBed, Film Supply, and Stills—agrees that music, video and photography need the human touch. While AI can impact companies like MusicBed, it is the *creator* who can thrive during the AI revolution.

Would a concert be standing room only to hear AI sing and play music? Not a chance. We connect with the artists, their emotions, and the stories behind their work. Can musicians utilize AI to speed the creation process? Absolutely. But again, AI is enhancing our creative abilities, not replacing them.

AI Ethics

One of the biggest issues many have with AI is the legal aspects. As I mentioned in talking about branding, AI cannot be copyrighted, but that isn't stopping people from using it. Artists are harshly against the use of AI because it can bring the risk of stealing copywritten material.

Class action lawsuits have been filed against OpenAI and Meta for infringing upon copywritten material. Silverman's lawsuit accuses them of scraping the contents of her *Bedwetter* autobiography to train their AI systems. Actors and actresses have been critical as well, fighting to keep their own voices from being used in AI simulations.

On the flipside, the estate of James Earl Jones is open to the idea of letting AI replicate his voice. Can you imagine what Darth Vader would be like without his voice?

Getty Images is a big players in the creative realm. MusicBed and Adobe are playing catch-up with companies like Canva. Their big issue is copyright. Their libraries reflect human art and creativity. When an image, font or song is used, the company makes money but also gives payouts to the original artists. AI engines remove the original artist from the equation, essentially enhancing the term "starving artist." These companies are a huge support to artists and do not want to cut them out. Getty and Adobe have created their own AI libraries, at the same time, working on algorithms to track and attach AI-created imagery to original artists. So if I were to create an image, download and purchase it, any photo or piece of art used to create the image would warrant a commission. I then would have a legitimate copyright of the image.

Just like with a brush stroke to put paint on a canvas, leaders of AI use a sequence of keystrokes to create something memorable and unique. AI will be like hiring someone to do imperfect preliminary work to save the real artist a lot of time. AI can be trained, retrained, and fired whenever needed. It will never be the perfect solution, but when utilized correctly, it can expedite the production by talented artists.

Utilizing new tools and strategies to developing robust processes will only lead to success. It is not something to be scared of, but it is something that should inspire excitement and innovation.

Points to Ponder

- Use AI as a powerful business tool: AI will never replace human creativity, but it has the potential to revolutionize business process, providing entrepreneurs with tools to solve problems, innovate, and streamline operations.
- Let AI help improve business strategies: While AI cannot do our thinking for us, it can be an effective brainstorming to immediately present possibilities that might otherwise be missed.
- Be aware of ethical and legal liabilities: Legal frameworks around AI usage are still evolving. Use resources that will protect you from copyright infringement and displacement of artists.

The Art of Using Distractions

I've already said a lot about how to encourage creativity and ways to push your imagination. Now, let's look at achieving positive results by using our distractions—the activity forces that might hinder your creativity.

Movies and Television

In late 1800s, if a U.S. resident wanted to know what China was *really* like, photos and books weren't sufficient. You had to book passage on a steamship, spend well over a month getting there, and then tour cities by rickshaw and walk through the countryside for a year. Even then, you might know what we now can see in a few hours of movies and television. Everybody knows that's a remarkable improvement, unless we stop to think about what we've lost.

Do movies function as leeches, sapping the life out of creativity, or are they sources of inspiration? In the years before electricity, we had oil lamps for reading at night. Books were good if you knew how to read and write. Schooling was limited by the need to work the farms, so people often spent evenings in the parlor. From the words they heard Grandma or Mom read about life in China, they had to create all the pictures, sounds, and actions with their own imaginations. A decade later, they had radio shows with voice actors and sound effects, which was more entertaining because they didn't have to imagine as much. Finally, with movies and television, we hardly have to imagine anything more than just believe we're part of the action we're watching.

Is this proof that movies and television are creativity leeches? Not necessarily, but you have to make it about more than just entertainment. An amazing amount of creativity went into every scene. Creative people are responsible for making reality shows appear real. Therefore, movies are a grand form of artistic expression. Their stories have the ability to inspire, motivate, and stir creativity inside us in new ways.

To stimulate creativity, you must look behind the scenes—the plot, characterization, and acting. What was said and why? What wasn't said? What parts are captivating? Why? What caused some parts to be boring? How could the movie have been made better? Did you notice the parts that weren't believable?

As a teenager, I watched movies like *The NeverEnding Story* fantasy over and over because of how much it stirred my imagination. I wanted to live in that world or be Atreyu. I dreamed of being Bastion and riding on the back of Falcor, the furry dragon.

Hours and hours spent dreaming fantasy was a reality. All dreams are birthed with an idea that pushes creativity in many directions. Without realism and believability, fantasy stories would be meaningless. Thus, we must be creative to translate the impossible and improbable into a world of reality never before seen. Do you see a parallel here?

With practice, we can use this kind of ability to

fantasize the impossible and improbable in our enterprises and then think of ways to make previously unconsidered possibilities into something others can believe and accomplish.

The Hero's Journey

About the time we think our hero might succeed, something else goes wrong. Now, he's in even bigger trouble, and the situation demands a much greater sacrifice. Maybe he isn't our hero at all, and somebody else must save the day. Success comes only after repeated failures and short-lived dreams that turn to nightmares. Sounds a little like the business world, doesn't it?

Entrepreneurs dare to become heroes by failing their way to success, by relying on others to help save the day, and believing they can find a solution when nobody else does.

The hero's journey is doing more than just a *job*. That's boring. True adventure comes from accomplishing more. What will it be? How will you get there? If your venture is exhilarating, filled with ideas, creativity, and excitement, you're an entrepreneur. You thought you could conquer the world. Become the hero. But now you must overcome all the impossible situations. If the journey is easy, you can't be the hero.

In the *Lord of the Rings* movie, the lowliest of people become the saving grace for Middle Earth. The hobbit Frodo Baggins must battle inward turmoil as much as the external war. Early on his journey, Frodo loses his protector to a demon monster. Soon, he understands what he must do—continue his venture on his own. Little did he know that those closest to him would walk with him on the road ahead.

In your ventures, you need many creative people supporting your efforts. But in the end, your own creativity is most crucial. You are the leader because you must make the hard decisions. It's part of the Art of Entrepreneurs and what makes you the hero.

The Creative Process

The hero's story is as much about the process of overcoming obstacles as it is about the prize and lesson learned at the end. The same is true in the business world.

Without the process, a business stagnates, can't keep up with changes in society and the marketplace, and becomes insignificant. As with a journey from one state to another, there are many ways to get there. With creativity, we adjust for detours, road hazards, and traffic delays. Without creativity, we trust our GPS. We may sit parked on the road, waiting for something to happen and hoping for the best, which makes us victims instead of victors.

The creative process is continually looking for a better way, building on past failures and successes. We learn costly lessons that are valuable because we now know what *not* to do. Some roads are longer and more difficult than others, but they all must lead to the fulfillment of our vision.

Note to Self

When asked what advice I would give to my younger self, I said, "My advice would be *nothing*." You may have heard that hindsight is better than foresight, but actually, that statement is irrelevant. We can't change the past, and even if we could, the future wouldn't be what we think it would be. So I thought *nothing* was a good answer.

I can't give advice to my younger self. What I *can* do is make notes to my present self as I consider what I've learned from the past and think creatively about what my future might be.

Sometimes, people waste their creativity by wishing they had done things differently. This is what I call the "if only" diseases. If only I had invested wisely, I would be worth millions. If only I had bought that stock *before* it quadrupled in value, I could be a millionaire. If only I bought bitcoin in the beginning, I could be a billionaire. If only I had taken that other job, I wouldn't have to deal with all these problems. Even if our hindsight were true, and it most probably isn't, we can do nothing about it. Saying *nothing* to our younger selves is better than living in regret.

Count Positives

With regret, we make the past worse than it really is. The antidote for the "if only" disease is changing your focus from all that went wrong or could have been better to all the positives. So you learned costly lessons, but now you know what *not* to do. This is good.

The more you focus on the good things from the past, the more creative you can be to enjoy a greater measure of success. You should not forget the struggles and failures that brought you to where you are, but you need to use them as steppingstones, not stumbling blocks.

One of the best examples of this is celebrating weekly wins. Something simple but impactful as a business leader is to send out a weekly email to the team. You may have weekly meetings, but there is something different about a weekly highlight email—especially when you include the weekly wins. Highlight new projects, employee successes, and anything else to pump up the team.

For almost five years, I have been sending weekly emails to the team, and the impact has been significant. I share a piece of information about the business that might not come up in meetings. For example, talking about culture, the impact of financial stress like the economy, new technologies like AI, or anything that impacts the business. Highlighting their wins creates a level of support and trust they don't see anywhere else. Lastly, when team members acknowledge one another's wins, their enthusiasm rises to a much higher level. Everyone loves getting an update from the "boss man" every week, to learn what is going on within the company.

I often get responses to my emails with comments like: *Thank you for the shout out. It feels good to get a few wins like that!* What a boost to company morale. The more you encourage and support your team, the more they will support you in return. I challenge you to try a weekly email for a month and see what happens.

Living in the "if only" disease is doomed to failure because success is an impossible dream. Really? Yes, and let me tell you why: no matter how much success the entrepreneur has, we're compelled to think creatively, looking for something even better. If we can't count the positives, share them and appreciate where we are now, we're hindering our ability to move forward.

Social Media Numbness

If we're not careful, smart phones can make us embarrassingly dumb, and social media can isolate us from the activities that are crucial for our success. Like any useful tool, the value is all about how our tools are used.

For those who spend hours scrolling through endless posts, social media can be the greatest time-suck of their work week. I should know. Guilty as charged, so I have to be careful. One picture leads to the next, and so on. As soon as I browse more than I contribute, I know I have a problem. Time to step away and do something worthwhile.

Cell phones and social media should be a means for you to share your creativity, not to get lost in unimportant stuff. A few years ago, I wanted to paint something every week, but it wasn't happening. Several months later, a friend challenged me to take a serious look at how I was spending my time.

Seeing friends' photos brought joy and satisfaction. TikTok and Facebook posts now have even more appeal with videos that cause us to lose track of time. They just feel good, and we want more. What appeals to you on

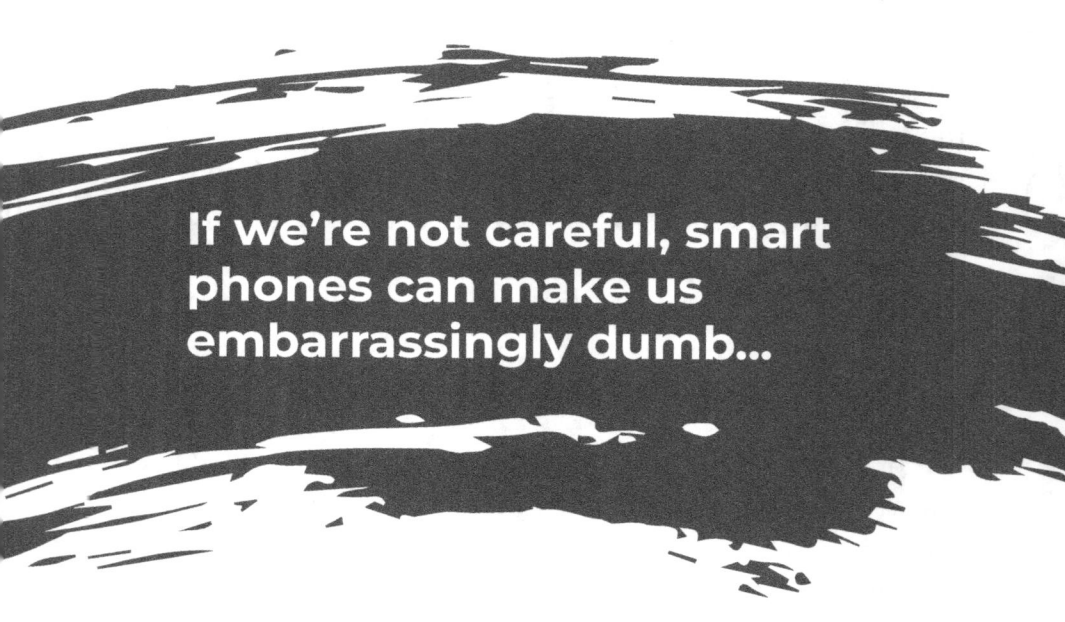

If we're not careful, smart phones can make us embarrassingly dumb...

social media? Watch out. Under the guise of being helpful, posts can be creativity killers. For example, I can be sucked into a video of African wildlife, or I might be invited to the next new, really cool, video game. An hour goes by before I realize it, an hour wasted with nothing to show for it.

Video Games

Those who make their living designing video games need to spend a lot of time playing, thinking creatively about what new and exciting application could be developed. Looking at how characters move and interest with the environment is a key part of development. But for the rest of us, video games are seen as a time suck, a way to isolate ourselves from the outside world.

Video games are addictive because we don't notice the danger while we bask in endorphin-filled pleasures outside the stresses of everyday life. Games can be a limited help with creativity, but for most part, they are simply a means to get lost.

My problem is becoming so lost in the game that I can't stop with one level. I don't want to quit until I win, so I keep playing until I'm into the next level. Winning was such a thrill, I just have to see if I can meet the next challenge. Hours pass like minutes, and before long, I wonder where the night went.

Reality becomes a blur when a video game becomes your life. Any creative skills gained from playing is now useless, because you are disconnected from the needs of a real enterprise. Like people living in Facebook rarely speak to someone face-to-face, some gamers can miss the human interactions that would make their creativity explode.

On the opposite side of the spectrum, video games can stimulate creativity, within limitations. Games today are full of stories and journeys with triumphs and failures. Each road leads to a new challenge, another obstacle to overcome.

If you can grasp business journey like a video game, your failures can become the fuel to the fire that completes the task. As a kid, I played a game called *Rygar*, one of the best old NES games. The ending was especially difficult. I spent hours navigating the world to get to the final boss, only to lose and restart at the last checkpoint, which meant another hour of playtime. While frustrated, I was determined to win. Then I failed again. Finally, after hours and hours of failure, I beat the final boss and won.

As you must experience and know, defying the odds and winning at great cost is an indescribably great thrill.

This game was interesting because the final boss was easy to defeat—once I knew how. Yes, it took a long time to get there, but learning how was the essential part of the story.

In the business world, we try and fail. The sense of having to start over is unavoidable, part of the cost in winning. Overcoming that obstacle, and most importantly, how to do it again, moving forward, is essential for success.

Video games might be a waste of time, but they also can inspire you to achieve great things through failure.

Music Magic

Like video games, for some, music is an escape from reality and does nothing to stimulate creativity. But properly utilized, music can provide welcome support for creativity and innovation.

Something about the way our brains are wired causes music to help us remember words we would otherwise forget. The best example of this is children learning. For two years, we homeschooled our twins through Classical Conversations. During their elementary years they learned what is called the "timeline" song, which begins in Week 1 with the Age of Ancient Empires (Creation to c.450 AD).[3] Week after week, new information was added and repeated. By the end of the year, key points in the

---

3   https://fiveintheforest.com/classical-conversa-tions-timeline/

timeline were remembered and served as a foundation to people, events, and dates in history. Ten years later, the twins can roll through pieces of the song without hesitation, flowing with the musical tone throughout.

Grueling work can be made pleasant with music playing in the background. TV ads incorporate music because the right tune adds a positive feeling about the product and increases sales. We become better producers when we can whistle while we work.

Music can be a creative leech if we choose music that we find boring or don't particularly care about. But a tune with a beat can synchronize your thoughts and help your creativity. Build yourself a playlist that fits the pace of your work.

Certain types of music can cause a shift in your brain waves associated with meditation and sleep states. Choose wisely, and what otherwise might be a distractive leech can instead boost your creative thinking so you can continue the journey of unlocking your creative genius.

Indra Nooyi, former CEO of PepsiCo, offers an interesting perspective on how embracing creativity and art can positively impact business leadership. Nooyi is known for her innovative approach to leadership, which includes incorporating elements of art and music into her business strategies.

Nooyi has spoken about how she used visualization techniques inspired by art to help her team better understand complex business concepts. For example, she sketched out ideas during meetings, turning abstract financial or strategic concepts into visual representations.

This approach helped her team grasp and remember key ideas more effectively.

She encouraged creativity at PepsiCo by promoting "design thinking" across the organization. She believed that design was not just about aesthetics but also about problem-solving and innovation. Under her leadership, PepsiCo invested in design-led innovation, which led to the development of new products and packaging that better met consumer needs.

She also used music as a tool for leadership and team building, sometimes using song lyrics or musical metaphors to convey important messages. This approach not only made her messages more memorable but also helped create a more engaging and creative work environment.

The impact of Nooyi's creative approach was significant. During her tenure as CEO from 2006 to 2018, PepsiCo's sales grew by 80 percent, and the company expanded its portfolio of healthier food and beverage options, demonstrating both financial success and innovative thinking in response to changing consumer trends.

Points to Ponder

- Use movies and TV to boost creativity: To avoid creativity leeches, critically engage the plot, characters, and believability to understand the purpose and technique in their creation.
- Avoid "if only" regret thinking: Dwelling on past mistakes and missed opportunities are creativity killers. Build on lessons learned and move forward with creative confidence.
- Celebrate successes: Recognizing small wins within a team fosters trust and motivation, encouraging more creative endeavors and greater success.

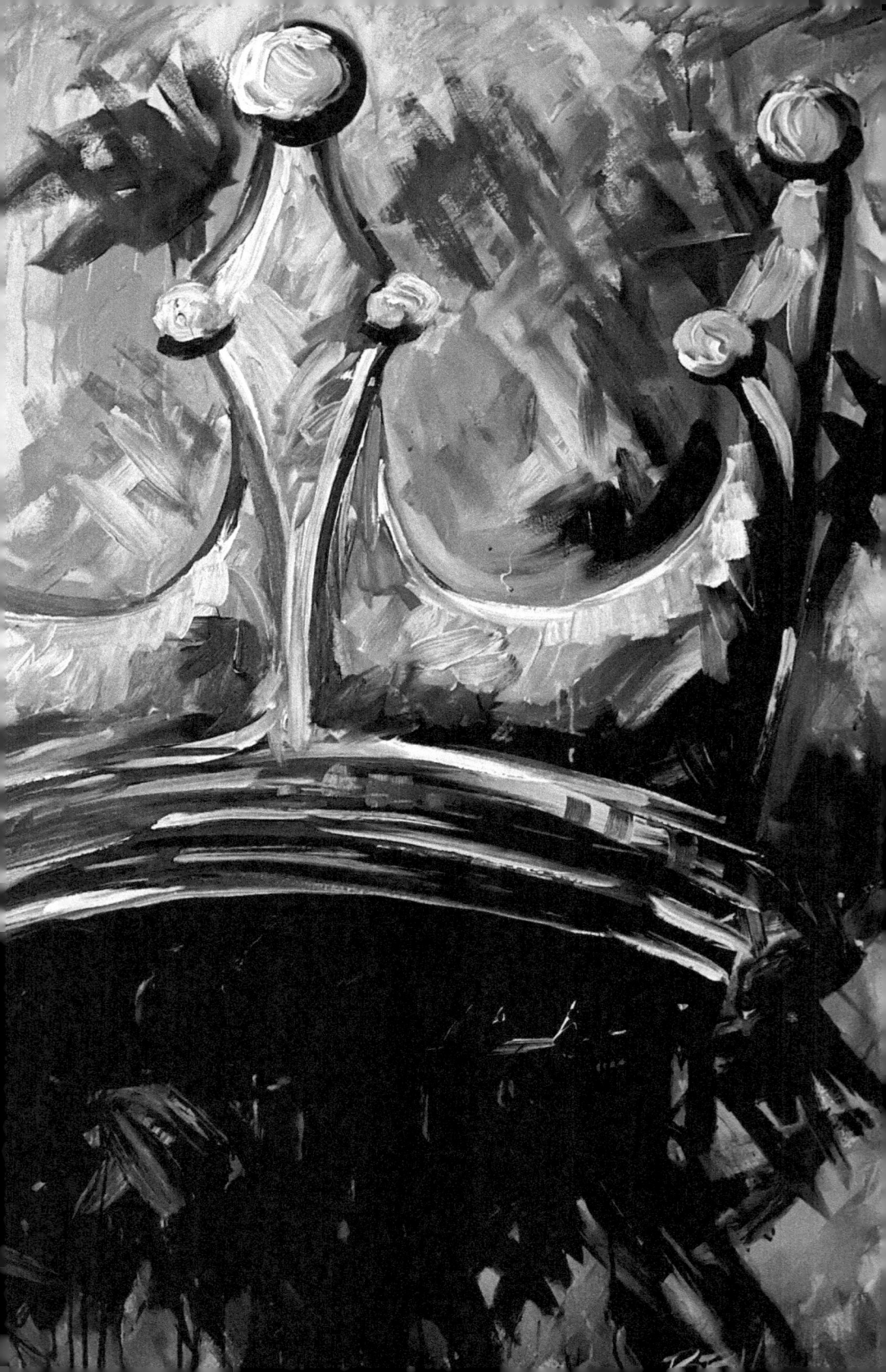

The Art of Success

Success is rarely a stroke of luck or a sudden turn of fate. It's often the culmination of relentless effort, unseen dedication, and a steadfast commitment to a vision.

Full-Court Press

This need to push forward is particularly evident in the stories of individuals like Alex Hormozi and Mr. Beast. Despite their current fame, they spent years away from the limelight, honing their crafts and persistently pushing forward.

Apparent overnight successes can sometimes take twenty-five years to develop.

Before becoming a celebrated entrepreneur, Alex Hormozi went through numerous tests and trials that would have defeated all but the most committed, determined individuals. His journey is a testament to the power of resilience and the importance of learning from failure. His success story underscores the fact that success is built on a foundation of hard work and continuous improvement.

Similarly, Mr. Beast started as a relatively unknown content creator. He spent years producing videos that reached a relatively small audience. His early work was a far cry from the viral hits he produces today. But it was through this rigorous process of content creation, learning from audience feedback and adapting his approach, that honed his unique style. His rise to fame is not just a story of creativity but also of patience and persistence.

Both men's stories exemplify the truth that there is no shortcut to lasting success.

In a social media age where influencers seem to rise overnight, the years of hard work and perseverance aren't recognized for their contribution to eventual breakthroughs.

For Alex Hormoza and Mr. Beast, a great success was just the beginning of a new and better journey. They continue to work tirelessly, understanding that the landscape is ever-changing, because what brought them success initially might not be sufficient to sustain it.

The path to success is never a quick trip. It's a marathon, not a sprint, not only demanding talent and creativity but also resilience, adaptability, and a long-term perspective. The secret to marathon magic is never giving up, having a relentless commitment for doing whatever it takes.

Eventually, we may step into the spotlight and shine, but in the meantime, we press forward in the darkness.

A Pattern for Others

Being a leader can only mean one thing. It's right there in the word: *lead*. So part of your success formula must include such value that people will trust your vision and want to follow.

Without a shared vision, you get to walk alone.

Financial Stability and Wealth

You don't have to own the world, but you do need the resources to take the next profitable step. No matter how much you have, it's not enough when you can't afford the risk to take the next right step.

Business Success

You know you've built something worthwhile when you're not needed for day-to-day operations. You're successful when the business can do just fine without you, and your value comes from your creativity and imagination for further growth.

Retirement

Freedom from responsibility is wonderful when you're ready to die. Or when you want to be someone having a lot but be of little value in serving others. Colonel Sanders was 62 years old when he founded Kentucky Fried Chicken, a wonderful age to retire from a service station serving meals to travelers to franchising the most delicious farmland recipe.

True entrepreneurs never die. They just retire so they can do something greater.

Family and Relationships

Raising good children and spending quality time with family are deeply personal and fulfilling aspects of success. They reflect a balance of personal and professional life and a commitment to familial responsibilities.

As a business leader, understanding the connection between home and work life is important. What happens in the home directly impacts performance at work, and the reverse is true, as well. When your team members have stability and support at home, their productivity and engagement at work naturally improve. If their home is in shambles, guess what? That chaos will be reflected in their work.

Achieving balance isn't just about time management—it's about creating an environment where employees feel supported in both aspects of their lives. Flexibility, empathy, and understanding from leadership go a long way in maintaining this balance.

In his book *The 7 Habits of Highly Effective People*, Stephen Covey talks about the importance of "Sharpening the Saw." This idea is about regularly renewing and balancing key areas of your life—physical, social/emotional, mental, and spiritual. If you neglect these areas, you burn out, and that affects both your personal and professional life.

Covey also talks about Win-Win thinking, where mutual benefit is key, whether in relationships or balancing work and home life. The takeaway is clear: real success comes from finding balance. You can't thrive at work if you're neglecting your personal life.

His message is simple. If you take care of your personal wellbeing and relationships, you'll be more effective as a leader and more successful in your work. Both parts of life are connected. If you nurture them, you'll see the benefits in both areas.

Think of your team as a great piece of art requiring constant adjustment and attention to detail. Encouraging a healthy balance for your team will lead to stronger, more-creative, and more-committed individuals. It's not about achieving perfection. It's about fostering an environment where work and life coexist in a way that leads to personal fulfillment and professional success—for the overall success of everyone.

Travel

The ability to travel, both for business and pleasure, says you are successful enough to enjoy life. Unlike some millionaires who struggle because they don't yet have enough, successful entrepreneurs can enjoy every day at work and at play, as if they were always on vacation.

Time Management and Flexibility

Having control over your time, with the flexibility to engage in activities you value and balance necessities with electives are key success indicators.

We easily get so caught up in building for the future that we lose sight of what we're missing today. When that happens, it's a good time to step back, take a deep breath, and restore some of your childlike imagination and creativity.

In retrospect, nobody wishes they had spent more

time making money. What people really want is more time with their loved ones. It's not just about how much we earn or how much recognition we gain. Life isn't found in the abundance of our possessions. The moments we spend with family and friends build relationships that we can remember and cherish forever.

No deathbed confession ever said, "If only I had made more money ..." No, but you will hear someone say, "I wish I'd spent more time with my family." Make sure you're spending days with the right people, doing what really matters.

The Artist's Way

No matter how you define success, you'll never get there without focus and determination. With a wonderful goal and a perfect plan to get there, the journey will have twists and turns and detours you could never anticipate, not in a million years.

In the artist's way, creativity and innovation are crucial. You have to be agile and flexible, always ready to make adjustments.

I never set out to be an entrepreneur. My goal wasn't to make money. The Number One goal for me was to help people. My dream was to help clients fulfill their dreams. Even more than my own success, I'm most thrilled when I can contribute to the success of others.

True artists find pleasure when others are rewarded by their work.

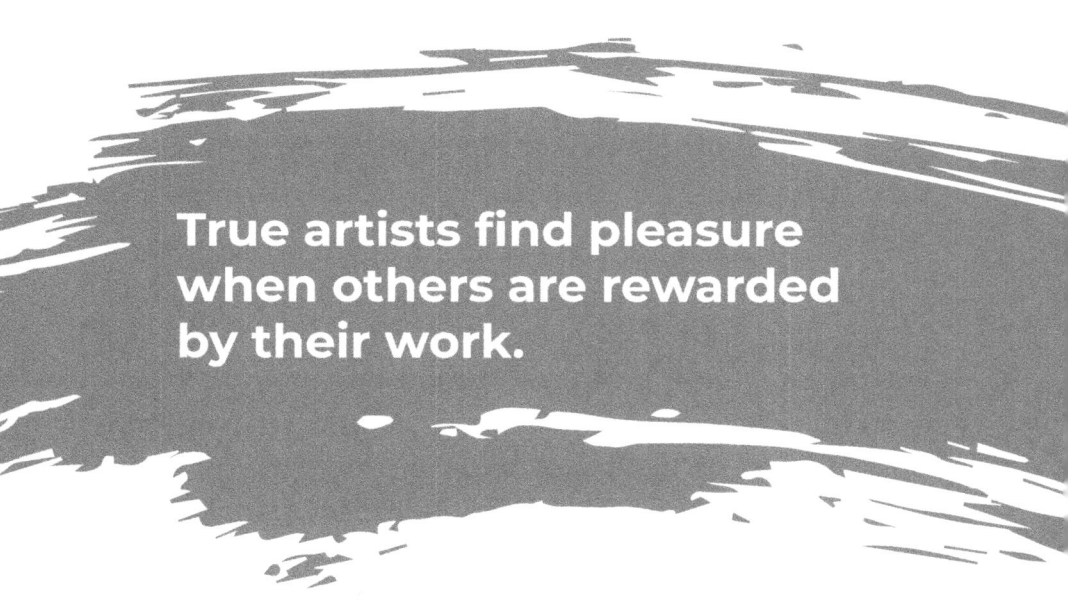

True artists find pleasure when others are rewarded by their work.

The End in Mind

When artists plan to begin a painting, they have an outcome in mind. Not always knowing where to start, but knowing where to go is key.

My creativity is challenged. Where do I start? Will it be good enough? What will I do if something goes wrong? What colors do I use? More question come ... more than I can possibly answer.

With the first brush stroke, I'm committed. No turning back now. We'll see what develops. I must keep moving forward, making adjustments wherever I mess up.

This process can take hours, days, or even months. With each brush stroke, with each added color, I'm one step closer the moment I can step back and appreciate the pain and strain necessary to complete the finished painting. I know where I want to go, so I keep going, never letting a little "mistake" hold me back from the success that lies ahead.

Does a chess player know exactly how the game will be played? No, not even if he's playing himself. Fresh ideas create new situations that could never be anticipated. We visualize the future but must then respond to what actually happens. Win, lose, or draw, opposing strategies are in play. There is an art to each strategy. Who will win? That depends on how well we play the game.

Bobby Fisher, the grandmaster of chess who defeated Boris Spassky in 1972, could visualize twenty moves ahead. Because of the complexity of so many possibilities, some think he could anticipate a hundred different moves under various possibilities. But he still had to play the game, or he had no chance of winning. He still had to survive his past losses.

Establish worthwhile goals. Plan your strategy and plot your steps, one move at a time, one dollar at a time. With patience and persistence, your success will create a masterpiece that others can appreciate.

Success can be different for everyone. For some, success is driven by money. For others, it can be personal recognition or acclaim. Maybe spending time with people is most important.

One of my favorite movies, *Big Fish*, tells a story of Edward on his deathbed. He told the most farfetched stories that seemed to be fairy tales. There was the circus ringleader who turned into a werewolf at night. Conjoined twins helped Edward escape capture. While the characters were not exactly as the stories told, they represented real people who showed up to honor Edward at his funeral. The cojoined twins were separate, identical twins in real life. There was a circus ringleader. The stories were farfetched fantasies, but the impact upon those lives he touched created a lasting legacy.

On my deathbed, how will I be remembered? Will I have left a lasting impact? Will I lead others to do the same? Will my creativity inspire others?

Exercise: Think about how you want to be remembered. Write those thoughts and set that as the goal that inspires your daily life.

Points to Ponder

- Commit to relentless effort: Success is built on years of hard work, perseverance, and dedication to the vision.
- Balance your personal life with work responsibilities: Professional achievements have little value without personal fulfillment spending time with family and friends.
- Leave a lasting legacy: A person's *net worth* is valued at how much a person has, but a person's *value* is measured by how much has been given for the benefit of others.

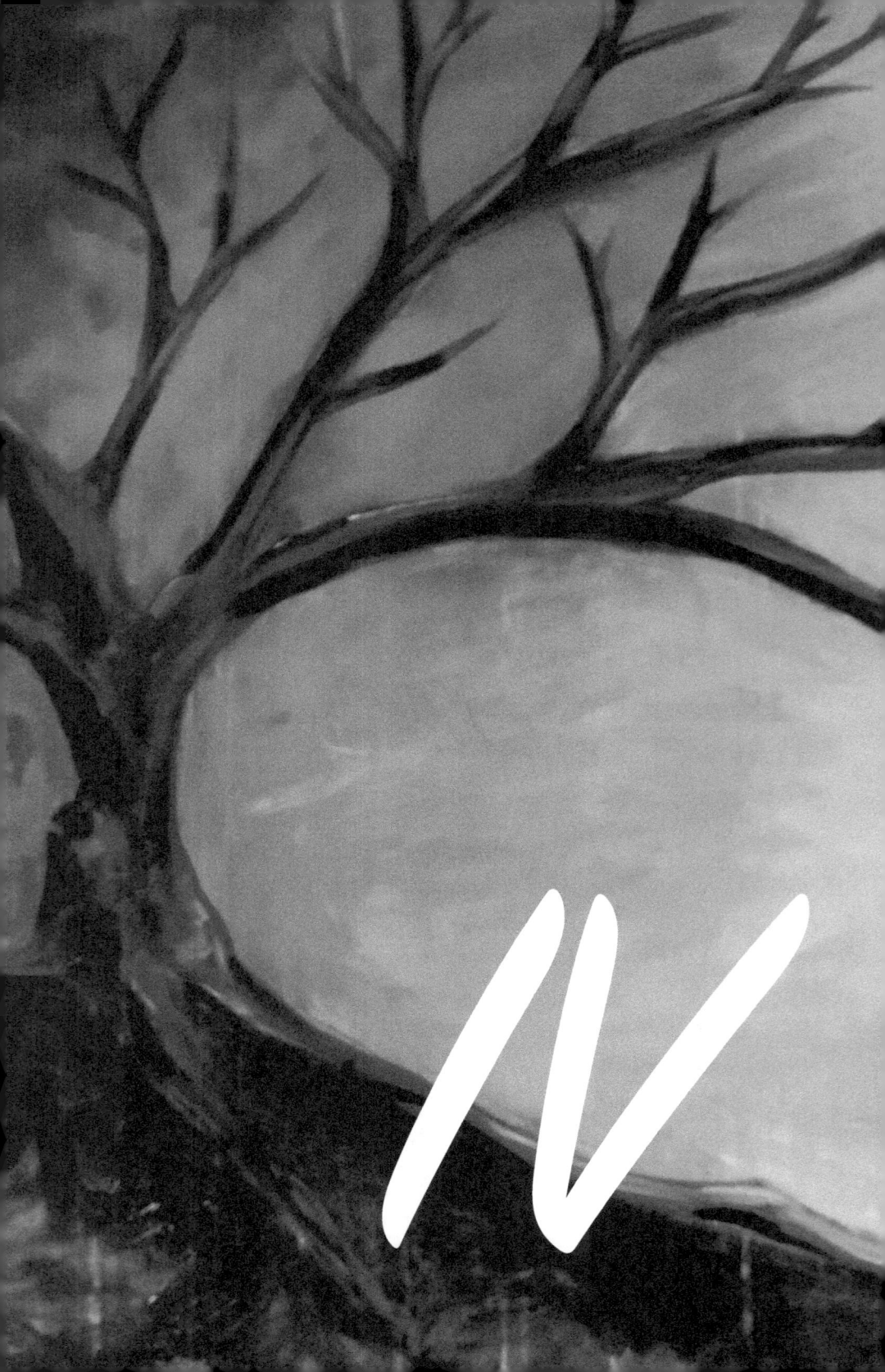

Crafting a
Masterpiece

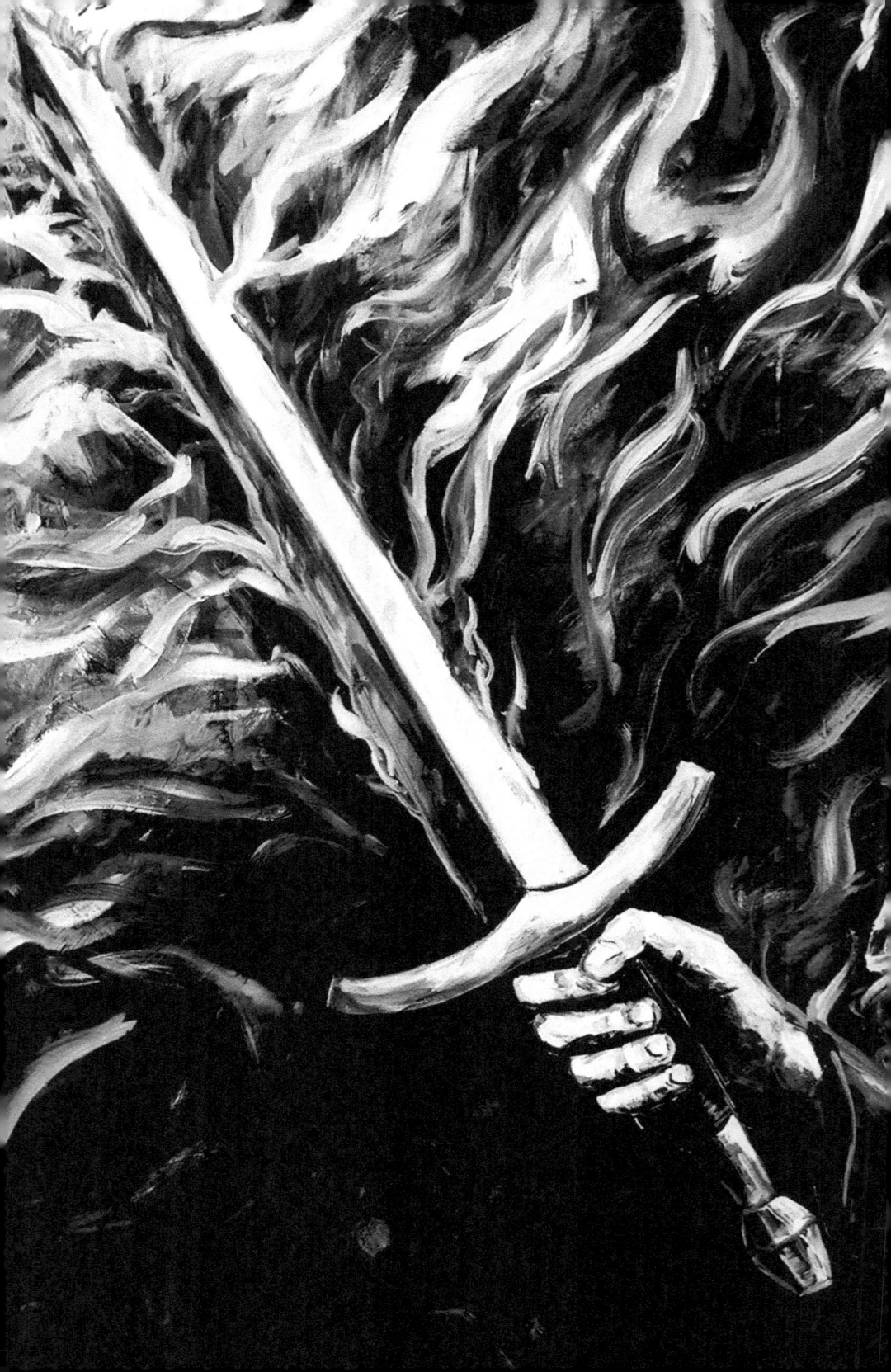

Unlocking Creative Potential

As an entrepreneur, you have the unique power to shape your business around your vision and values, creating ventures that not only thrive financially but also enrich your life and the lives of others. If your work isn't driving personal growth and fulfillment, it's time to reassess and realign. Unlocking your creative potential means tapping into a well of possibilities that can transform every part of your entrepreneurial journey. By embracing your creativity, you open doors, break through barriers, and uncover new opportunities. This creative awakening empowers you to reimagine your business and craft it into a masterpiece of innovation and purpose.

"Whether you think you can, or you think you can't—you're right." — Henry Ford

Fixed Mindset

Some people have a that's-just-the-way-I-am or it-is-what it-is mindset. They were born this way, grew up this way, and nothing is going to change them. With that belief, their abilities, intelligence, and talents are fixed. They aren't going to improve. What happens, happens, and nothing you do or say will change it.

Entrepreneurs with this mindset are not likely to experience much success. Because of our ever-changing marketplace and developing technologies, we must be ever-changing, always learning. Our old-style methods are sure to quit working so well.

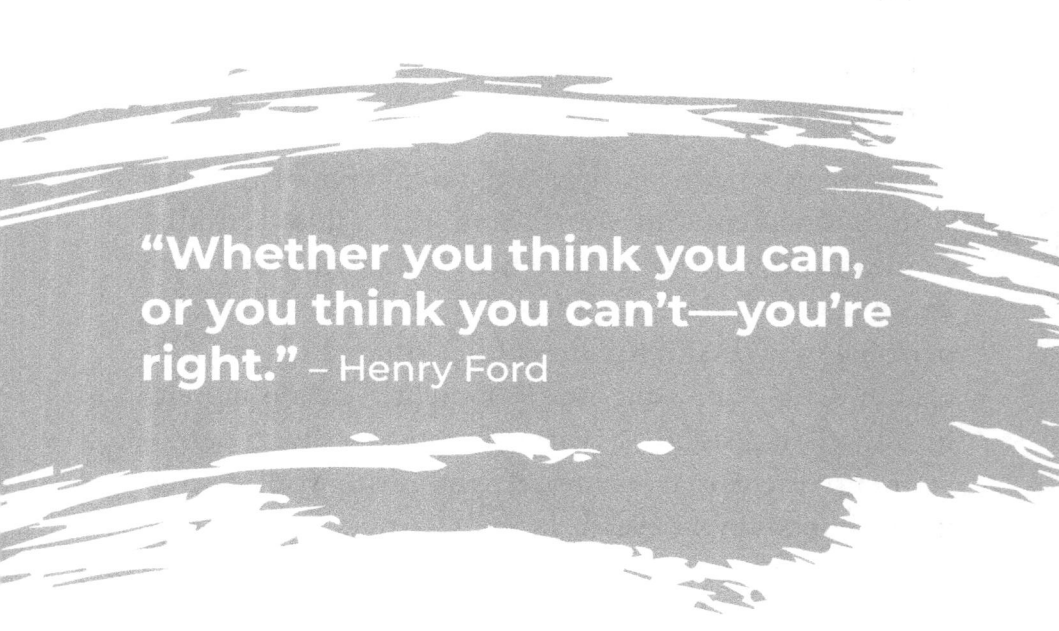

I saw this a lot with my dad. As creative as he was, sometimes his mindset was not of future possibilities. I cannot begin to count how many times I heard him say, "It is what it is." He spent twelve years researching the life of Christ and turning that research into a nonfiction book that read like a novel. It was a great and creative idea to share the Gospel story in a way that easy to read. After all that hard work, he the future of that book to "whatever happens, is going to happen." My dad may be an artist, but by his own admission, he is not an entrepreneur. He did not have the vision and mindset to see what needed to come next. He was boxed-in to what he could see moment.

Do you like to keep yourself in a box or do you want to be constantly growing and learning? Every entrepreneur I know is constantly learning and trying to expand their mindset. This is why business groups and masterminds are so popular. They know this is the ultimate way to succeed. If this is you, then you do not have a fixed mindset. If it is you, then get ready to wave at others flying by.

Personality Tests

For several years, we tested employees and applicants to understand their personalities, where their skills naturally fell, and what they liked and disliked. We used the Culture Index system to identify whether a new hire would be a good fit for the team. Were they a team player, visionary, with good social skills? Did they like or dislike dealing with details? My scores identified me as a social person who disliked details. That was partly true, but not entirely.

The tests proved helpful for our current employees because we better understood why performance was different for some, compared to others. For example, four employees had conflicting traits that said they were insecure, second-guessing themselves. One designer had problems starting a project and lacked confidence in bringing it to completion. Another designer worked on a project for a whole semester in college, redoing it several times, unable to decide whether it was good enough. They would start it, get it ready, second guess it, and start over. While this may have worked in college, in the real world, it was detrimental.

But there was a problem with the tests. They brought the assumption that character traits are *fixed* and cannot be changed. Since I'm not the person I used to be, I believe people can change, which was contrary to some of the tests. If an employee wants to improve, that desire will find a way, especially if we're able to provide the support they need.

Growth Mindset

Guiding employees and affirming our belief in their work have increased their self-confidence and helped them grow in their jobs. Having them take initiative and grow beyond the tests has exceeded more than we could imagine. Wait! We did imagine it. There is an art behind seeing the potential in employees and supporting them in who they can become. It is one of the most important things we can do in business.

Fixed personality tests are problematic because they fail to show a person's true potential. As a leader and artist, if you tell me I can't do something, I will most likely prove you wrong. But that trait didn't show up on my test.

In five years, I have seen two team members develop confidence and become more skilled in what they do— far beyond what I would have believed from the tests. This is why coaching, mentoring, and masterminds are so important. When team members are challenged to become the best version of themselves, and they are given reasons to want to, their mindset can change.

Yes, there are various personality tests, but how are you using them? Remember, your business isn't limited to just one test, but you must understand your team members. More importantly, do you know yourself?

After going through the test on my own, I recognized some of my strengths and weaknesses. In some ways, I was the problem, so I had to step back and let people do their jobs.

For example, I had a great idea. What did I do? I immediately left my desk to present my idea to members of the team. It was such a great idea, I couldn't wait. I needed to share it. Now! How many of us feel that way?

The problem was, I distracted my team from their work. Many on our team were task-oriented and wanted to be left alone to do their work. When I barged in to share my idea, I took them away from their focus. They became less productive and overly stressed. Generally, when the boss walks in, heart rates rise and people question why?

You are who you are, and only through personal development or coaching will that change. The good thing is, you can grow into a better creative version of yourself.

Check out these popular tests to start the process and learn more about yourself:

- Clifton Strengths Assessment
- DiSC
- Enneagram
- Culture Index

With great strategy, perseverance, and practice, what we like and dislike can change. People tend to excel at what they like, and they tend to like what they excel at. Is it the "like" or the "excel" that is weak? Strengthen that area, and work can be more fun than a vacation. Over time, both attitude and performance improve. That's the kind of growth you're looking for.

Most entrepreneurs have a growth mindset. Otherwise, they wouldn't have so many books, attend conferences, and participate in masterminds to learn more. That desire for improvement can be contagious whenever it is shared.

People who are hungry to succeed will find a way. With some encouragement, you might be amazed.

Creative Mindset

The growth mindset fosters a belief in the capacity for improvement and learning. A creative mindset builds upon this foundation by encouraging people to actively seek out new territories of thought and expression. Challenges are seen as opportunities to improve skills and generate novel ideas and solutions.

The creative mindset pushes people out of their comfort zones and sees failures as essential to achieve success. They want to question, explore, and challenge what they've been told by unlocking doors to imagination and ingenuity. That is, they not only grow within existing frameworks, but with their inventive minds, they also construct entirely new possibilities for the future.

The 2019 McKinsey study revealed that companies with a strong creative mindset significantly outperformed their peers in revenue growth and total shareholder returns. Organizations that prioritized creativity fostered a culture of innovation but also understood their customers, allowing them to adapt quickly to market changes.

By integrating creativity into our daily practices and decision-making processes, these companies influenced consumer behavior more effectively and maintained brand loyalty in an increasingly competitive landscape. Ultimately, they proved that a creative mindset is not just an asset but is a critical driver toward business success.

Here are some key aspects of the creative mindset:

- Curiosity: Seeking opportunities to learn and grow, they ask questions, explore new ideas, and are eager to understand the unknown.
- Open-Mindedness: Receptive to different perspectives and willing to challenge their own beliefs and assumptions.
- Adaptability: Embracing change and willing to modify an approach in response to new information or circumstances, which leads to more innovative solutions.
- Risk-Taking: Mistakes are a natural part of the learning process, and failures can be an essential open door leading to valuable insights and growth.
- Persistence: By maintaining focus and determination, never giving up, people overcome challenges and continue progress toward their goals.

- Reflection: Their own thoughts, experiences, and emotions are important self-awareness tools that help measure progress, identify areas for improvement, and provide learning experiences.
- Collaboration: By working with others, diverse perspectives can lead to new ideas and insights. Strong collaborative relationships foster a supportive environment that boosts creativity.
- Flexibility: Approach problems from different angles involves recognizing multiple solutions, being willing to change one's approach, and adapting to new information.

Nurturing Positive Traits and Habits

It doesn't matter the challenges some people may have. People are fully capable of developing a creative mindset that allows them to approach challenges with curiosity, resilience, and innovation. This mindset can be applied to various aspects of life, from personal pursuits to professional endeavors. It can lead to greater overall satisfaction and success.

Fostering exploration and pushing the limits of creativity will ensure future corporate development. This is why research and development are key to most businesses, especially in the tech world.

The more the creative mindset is pushed, the more ideas and opportunities will be created to move your organization forward. A creative mindset is a key to something even greater: discovering your inner artist and creative *genius*.

Here's a checklist for enhancing your mindset to be more creative:

- ¤ Practice regular reading: Stimulates the brain and exposes you to new ideas

- ¤ Keep a journal: Record creative ideas and reflect on them

- ¤ Engage in brainstorming sessions: Generate many ideas quickly without self-criticism

- ¤ Listen to music: Sets the right mood and can boost creativity

- ¤ Take regular breaks: Allows for mental rest and can lead to new insights

- ¤ Change your environment: New surroundings can inspire fresh thinking

- ¤ Meditate: Calms the mind and enhances focus

- ¤ Try lateral thinking exercises: Challenges fixed ideas and encourages new perspectives

- ¤ Ask questions: Cultivates curiosity and challenges assumptions

- ¤ Practice creative activities daily: Dedicate time specifically to creative thinking

- ¤ Collaborate with others: Exposes you to different viewpoints and ideas

- Continuously learn: Expand your knowledge base to make new connections

- Use mind mapping: Visually organize thoughts and see new connections

- Set creative intentions: Focus your mind on specific creative goals

- Try freewriting: Write without stopping to bypass internal censors

- Engage in physical exercise: Boosts overall brain function and can spark creativity

- Practice visualization techniques: Use mental imagery to explore ideas

- Embrace mistakes: View failures as learning opportunities

- Set ambitious goals: Challenge yourself to think bigger

- Stay flexible: Be open to changing your approach as needed

Remember, enhancing creativity is an ongoing process. Regularly practicing these techniques can help shift your mindset to be more creative over time.

Points to Ponder

- Develop a growth mindset: People can change, and entrepreneurs need to be example setters striving to improve their abilities, intelligence, and talents.
- Make personality test work for you: Tests can be useful to understand team dynamics but must include the right support and encouragement for corporate growth.
- Enhance creativity with collaboration: Diverse perspectives spark new ideas that will develop into valuable insights that will lead to long-term success.

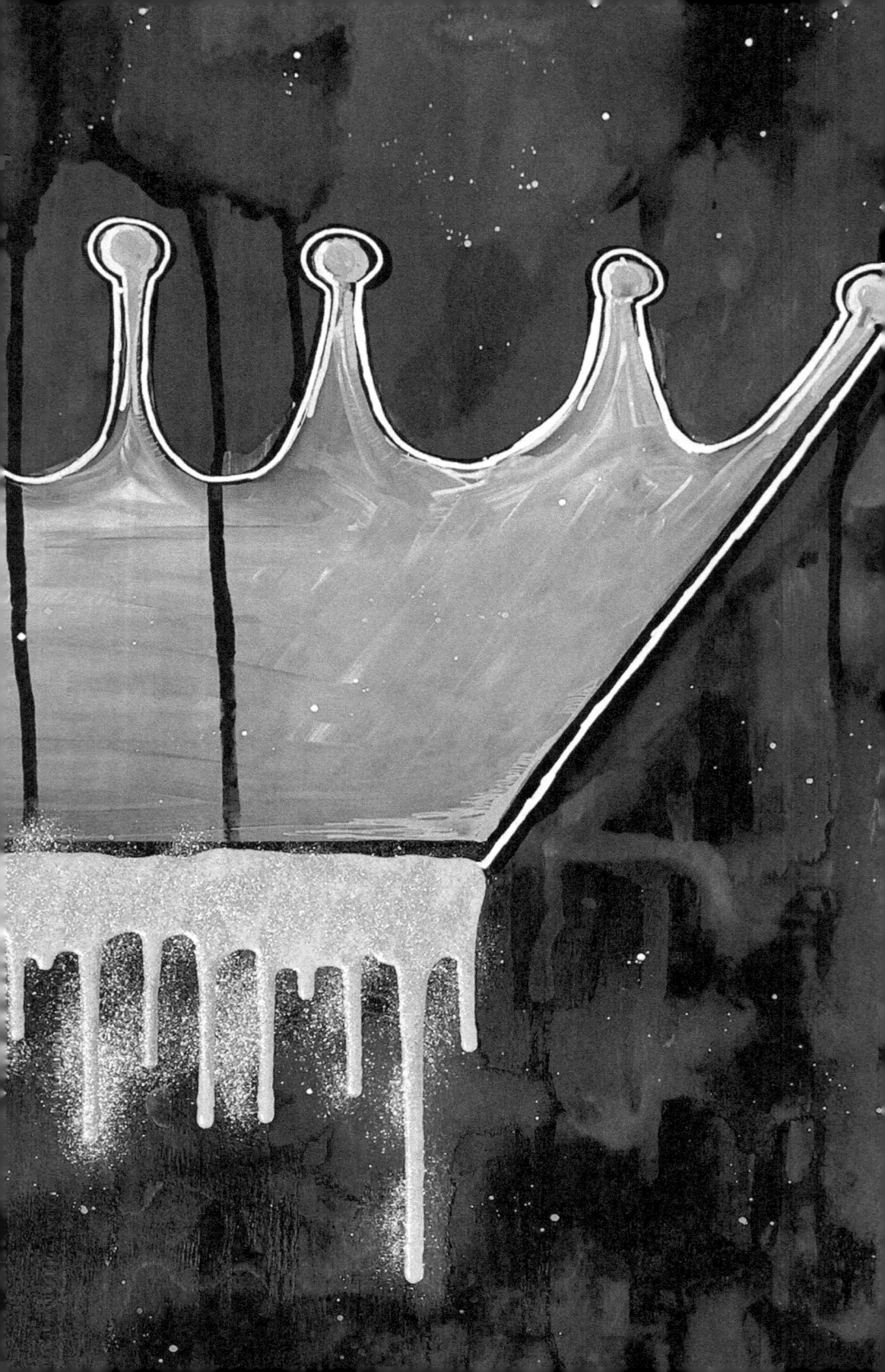

Dodging Entrepreneurial Pitfalls

Creativity is probably the main reason why you're successful, although you may not notice. As natural as curiosity is to a cat, so creativity is for the entrepreneur. Supposedly, curiosity can kill the cat. Creativity, with its wonderous ability to go where others have never ventured before, can make your life difficult. As a leader, you have to cast vision, look at goals, and foresee the various pitfalls ahead.

Pitfall Game by Atari

In the classic Atari video game called Pitfall, the character Pitfall Harry had to navigate through a jungle filled with hazards such as quicksand, crocodiles, and rolling logs. The game was simple and fun. Pitfall Harry seemed like a cross between Indiana Jones in search of the holy grail and Tarzan swinging through the trees to save Jane. In a limited amount of time, Pitfall Harry has to collect treasures while avoiding all the obstacles and enemies. Jump the logs, grab the vine, and swing over the pond with perfect timing. Or you get to start over.

Playing that game years ago may have helped me overcome many pitfalls in business. One day I'm jumping barrels and the next, I'm swinging over the pond, hanging on, not wanting to get soaked. I wasn't alone in this game. I had employees who were dealing with venomous snakes and stinging scorpions. As the gamer, my job was to anticipate the obstacles, prepare for problems, and help them navigate their journeys from one level to the next.

Dealing with Obstacles

Perhaps the most difficult obstacle to see and overcome was me. I could be the scorpion walking around like a constant devil's advocate, saying something will not work. I could be like the *Pitfall* barrel, overwhelming employees with problems that kept them from accomplishing their goals. Or I could be like the pond that people try to avoid so they can get their work done.

As the entrepreneur, I needed to be the game designer, seeing the whole picture and leading people in their respective roles. I needed to work *on* the business, but not *in* it. I had to adjust from being *in* the game to seeing the road to success, creating the best plan, and helping the team develop the processes that would take us to the next level.

Designing Instead of Being Played

Instead of being stuck in the day-to-day routine, I challenged my creative imagination to take the business to levels that I otherwise wouldn't have believed possible. My success depended on making others successful.

You are the architect of your life and your business. It can be a hard transition but one every entrepreneur must take, because through this transition, you will become the creative genius you were meant to be.

"Being played" says I've allowed myself to become the essential main resource for doing the work. That pitfall makes the business too much dependent on me, maybe thriving for a while, but the success can be short-lived. The business can weaken and die when it becomes too much to handle.

I played all the roles too often. If a project went sideways, I jumped in to fix it and saved the day. This brought success for me, but it didn't empower others to accomplish that much and more. If others couldn't do a better job than I could, I needed to ask why. Usually, they were capable and merely needed the training and experience that could only come by assigning the problem to them. If they weren't capable, then I needed to take a serious look at their future, whether they had A-level capability.

Professional Interrupter

Similar to being the savior, if I'm not careful, my creativity can be a liability, not an asset. Early on, when I had a stroke of creative genius, I walked around the office, interrupting what others were doing so I could solicit support. Bad idea. I soon learned that I was sidetracking others from the focus they needed to excel at their work, actually setting them up to fail.

Leading a team and recognizing that we all are players in the same game is a form of art. It doesn't matter where you are or what business you have, these roles play out the same.

Creating your own business can be the most exciting time in your life. Also the scariest. The possibilities are endless, especially if you are prepared in the beginning.

Hanging On Too Long

During my first five years of business in graphic design, I was a one-man show. I did the sales, creative work, billing, bookkeeping, and collections. In 2005, my partner and I founded Ardent Creative, Inc., and we hired our first employee. At the time, we didn't understand the value of mission, vision, and core values. We were focused on whatever needed to be done at the moment, which left little time for planning.

My five years of do-it-yourself habits were hard to break. I had to learn to trust others to do a better job than I could do. Problem was, they didn't always do things my way, and the work wasn't as good as what I could do. Or so I thought. Honestly, I was probably giving myself too much credit and wasn't giving my employees enough credit.

Employees didn't always meet my expectations. Oh, how tempted I was to take over and do the job right. Or I at least wanted to show them how—to micromanage. But no, if I did that, I would deprive them of the learning experience that I had gone through. I wanted to hang on. But tough as the choice was, I had to let go. I recognized my own failings to become who my team needed me to be.

Leading Through Failure

I used to say, "If you want something done right, you have to do it yourself." I could not have been more wrong.

When on the verge of losing my best client, trusting my team wasn't easy. Could I trust them as well as I trusted myself? If I took over and failed, I would easily forgive myself. My employees were hired because they could do a better job than I could. Why did I think their failure would be worse than mine? Ultimately, their failure could be better than my success because of what they learned through the process. Given the ability to lead themselves, they often exceeded my expectations. They thought of solutions that I never would have considered.

The book *Multipliers* by Liz Wiseman touches on different types of leaders, saying a person is either a multiplier or a diminisher. Multipliers are the rock stars who make everyone around them smarter and more capable. They're like, "Hey, I know you've got this," and create an environment where people can really shine and grow.

On the flip side, Diminishers are the energy vampires of the workplace. They think they're the smartest in the room and end up sucking the life out of their team's capabilities.

The book breaks down five key things Multipliers do: they attract talent, create space for others, challenge their team, encourage debate, and invest in their people's success.

Do you multiply the intelligence of the people around you, or do you diminish them? Are you a liberator or a tyrant? During the initial years of Ardent, I was not a great leader, and it diminished our growth. I was a diminisher.

Misguided Creativity

Looking back, I see that being a university art director was easy, but as a business leader, I needed to see various areas of business, not just paint on a canvas. Business leadership required a lot more creativity than I could have imagined. Even then, if I allowed myself to be too busy in daily operations, trying to be sure everything was done my way, I would never see the full potential of the business.

Trusting people and letting go can be risky, but it's the only way to achieve maximum potential. That's true for those who are new to the workforce or those who have been entrepreneurs for decades. Falling into complacency or fear can sneak into our daily activities without warning. Businesses that have been successful for a long time need new ideas and vision to keep pace with continual changes. Only well-guided creative leaders who learn how to be artists can anticipate the pivot points and trust others to make the right decisions.

Journaling

You may have heard that "out of sight is out of mind." Or stated another way, whatever great ideas you may have had will soon fall into the sea of forgetfulness, never to be remembered again. Yet those ideas could have developed into something profitable and lifechanging by simply taking time to write them down.

Everybody's memory can appear to be perfect, because we don't remember anything that we've forgotten. Okay, enough with the funniness. This is serious stuff.

If you aren't already doing this, start keeping a note-book. This isn't a notebook for client information. No, this is a notebook for yourself, either with ruled lines or plain sheets. Personally, I like journals *without* lines because sketching or doodling are ways I put ideas down. This required discipline, because it's so easy to forget when you're so busy. By the end of the day, so much has happened that your recent thoughts are already lost. There is no better time than *right now*, to preserve a thought for future use. I've heard that Einstein kept lots of notes because he didn't want to burden his mind with having to remember stuff. You know, he was a pretty smart guy.

Put your ideas, visions, and daily thoughts down on paper. Both good and bad. If you are like me, you may never go back and read them. Even that is okay, because just the process of writing it down will trigger your creative mindset. The more you do it, the more it will stir your creativity.

My good friend Tony Grebmeier developed the *Be Fulfilled* journal, a twelve-week guided program that serves as an excellent companion for building your dreams. I highly recommend it for setting and tracking goals, for offering reflections on your current position and future direction. It motivates users to reach their full potential and keeps daily progress records. Personally, I found it incredibly helpful in maintaining focus and achieving my own goals. You'll appreciate the boost it gives to start your journey.

Writing Genius

One great thing the journal pushed me to do was to write. Talent is overrated. So is genius. What matters is what we do to develop our talents. Keep doing that, and somebody will think you're a genius.

As a graphic artist, I didn't have much practice writing. Consequently, I never felt I was very good at it. I wrote when I had to, but journaling demanded a daily practice.

My writing was almost always last-minute to meet a deadline. In college, I had three weeks to write a junior-level English paper. But what should I write? I knew lots of words, but stringing them into meaningful sentences in a logical flow? I was struggling. The first day, I finished one paragraph. The next day, one more, and then another. After reading what I'd written, I had to start over. Day after day, I started with an idea and wrote a paragraph. Then I deleted it. Frustrated, I decided to work on it next week. That week passed with the same frustration. I wasn't getting anywhere until I was just forty-eight hours to the deadline. Then, what I couldn't accomplish in almost three weeks was finished in just a few hours. The pressure triggered my creativity, and I didn't have time to overthink every paragraph.

As an entrepreneur, I had to keep pressing forward with new ideas that had to develop one day at a time. Pulling everything together at the last minute wasn't going to work for me. This was another pitfall that required adjustment.

By writing something every day, my mind kept churning afterward. As I journaled, made sketches, and worked to stimulate my creativity, the ideas kept flowing, even while I was sleeping. Most people don't remember much of what they dream, but what I did remember said my mind was still at work, arranging pictures and processes in my mind. Almost magically, I woke up with solutions to problems I couldn't solve the day before.

As an entrepreneur, you need to lead with big dreams. The more you stir your creativity, the more you will dream. And the more you dream, the greater your potential for success. This is the Art of Entrepreneurs.

Artistic Challenge:

1. Start with journaling daily. This will help you both mentally and creatively.
2. Keep a notebook handy and write down ideas that randomly pop up.
3. Use a sketch book for your own drawing style, even if it's nothing more than stick figures.
4. Paint, draw, play a musical instrument, or build something creative every week.

Points to Ponder

- Trust the failure process: Allowing teams to fail leads to better long-term outcomes because members learn from their mistakes. Constantly stepping in to solve their problems stunts their growth.
- Write to unlock creativity: Daily writing helps entrepreneurs to think more clearly and capture valuable ideas.
- Allow others to take ownership: Entrepreneurs must learn to let go of doing everything themselves, even if things don't turn out well.

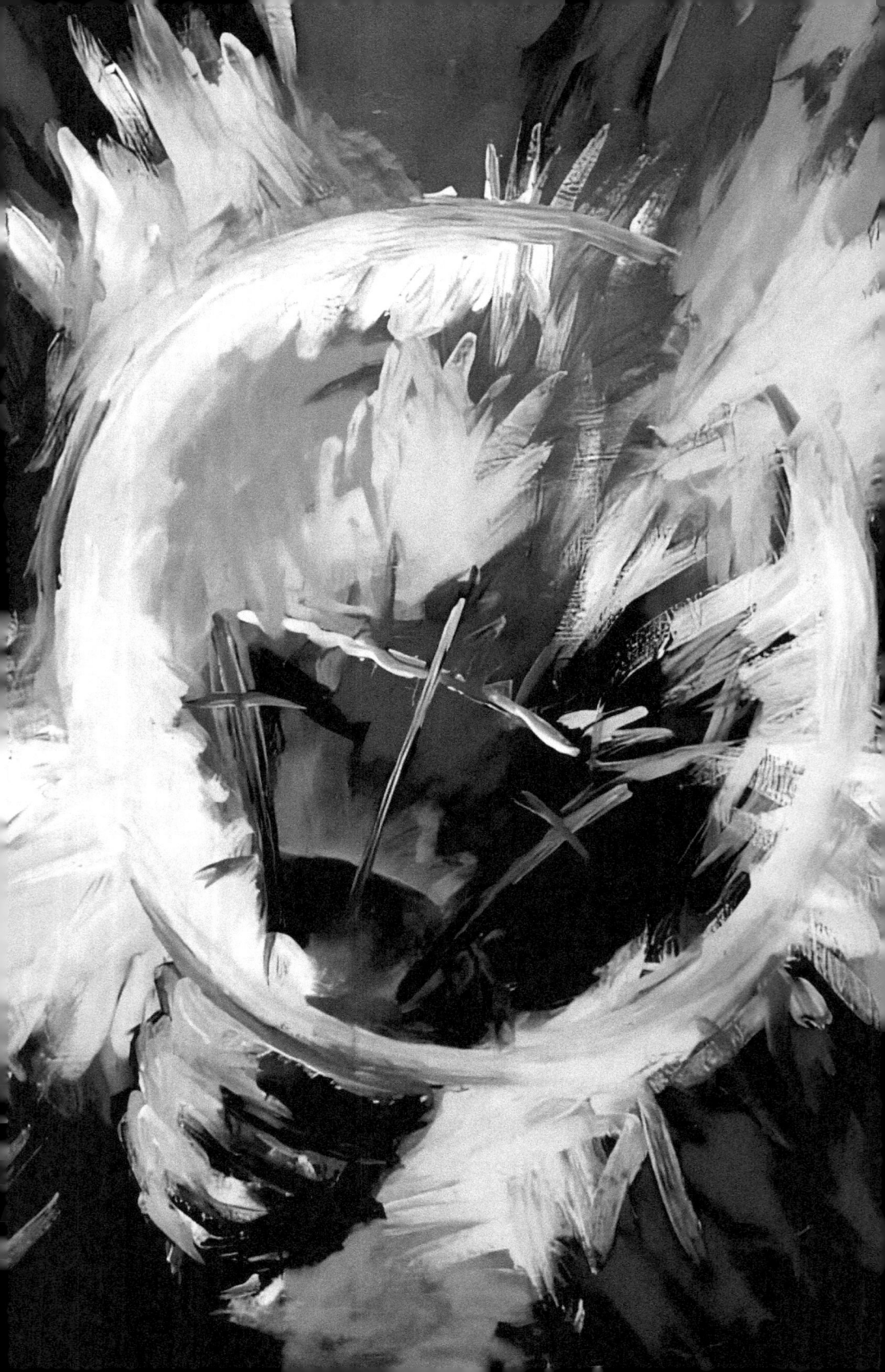

Navigating the Maze of Creativity

Renowned surrealist artist Salvador Dali emphasized the importance of dreams, imagination, and the work of the subconscious in the creative process. To explore new ideas, we must first break free from conventional norms. Striving for perfection could actually hinder creativity, so we need to embrace the imperfect and unpredictable. So we must challenge our imaginations to go beyond ordinary thinking.

Extraordinary Thought

Thinking "outside the box" means more than just daring to be different. It means broadening our perspectives to see reality beyond social norms. It breaks through impossibility thinking with the belief that impossibilities could be possible if we keep looking for solutions that others would swear cannot exist.

What the world has told us may not always be true. Even in science, current truths were later disproven by new knowledge. At one time, most people viewed the world as flat. There was the fear that if you sailed too far west, ships would fall off the edge of the world. If this were true, the ability to sail or fly around the world wouldn't be possible. But today, people who believe Earth is flat are just daring to be different. They aren't thinking outside the box.

Extraordinary thought doesn't ignore proven facts, it seeks to use those facts to discover new realities that haven't yet been considered.

The Maze

The Hampton Court Maze is part of a palace tour in Surrey, England, which invites visitors to explore its intricate network of hedge-walled paths that lead to dead ends. The goal is to find the center of the maze. Having to keep turning back and retracing your steps gives tourists a feeling of adventure and accomplishment. From the ground, the maze is challenging and might take thirty minutes, but from an arial view, the direct solution is a simple short walk. A maze printed on paper is different, with more twists and turns and more dead ends so the puzzle is challenging, even with an arial view.

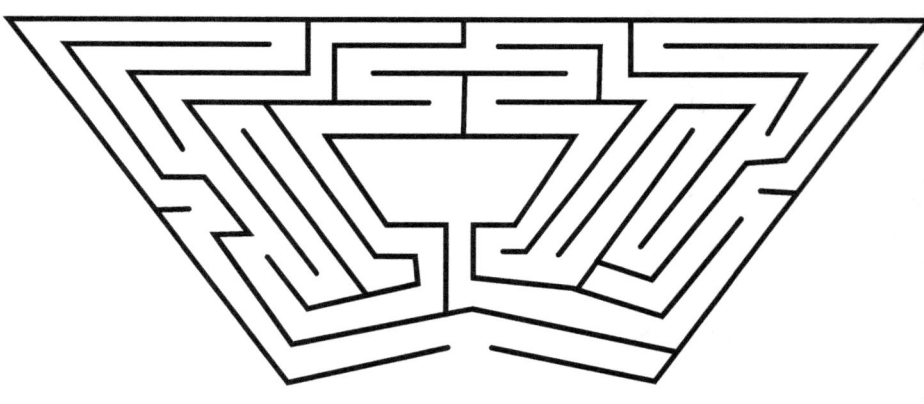

Illustration of the Hampton Court Maze

Solving a maze is all about perspective and visualization of a direct path to reach the goal. Practicing the puzzles on paper will challenge and stimulate your creativity to find solutions. In real life, you are lost inside the maze, with no real bearings except for your own memory and perceptions of where you've been and where you might need to go. With awareness and creativity, you learn to navigate the different halls and walls to reach the end.

In working a maze, you'll feel a little disoriented and confused, but this is good. Refocus and calm yourself. Conquering small challenges is great practice for quick, creative thinking when you're facing big obstacles in business.

Walls of Opportunity

No matter how difficult the maze, successful entrepreneurs see a wall as an opportunity to grow, pivot, and shift in new directions. You may need to take a few steps back to find the right path. At other times, you may need to go in a completely different direction. In business, some rules are meant to be broken.

Who said you had to go *around* the wall? Is there a way to fly over, dig under, or blast through? Is there a team member who can help with achieving a solution? This is where creative thinking becomes vital. The wall quickly becomes something to overcome, not something that forces us to take a costly detour.

The Obstacle Course

Walls are objects to scale. As an obstacle-course racer, I am challenged to overcome obstacles. Some are easier than others. A five-foot wall isn't that intimidating. But a ten-foot height takes more strategy and strength. Making it over the wall never ceases to be a great thrill.

As I face another wall, I might say, "Oh, great!" Which could have two entirely different meanings, one with apprehension, the other with eager anticipation. With sheer strength, stamina, and determination, I can say, "I've done it before. I can do it again." I can believe that, even if I haven't faced a challenge this big before.

My first race was the Tough Mudder, twelve miles that were all about training and teamwork. I completed most of the obstacles on my own, but a few were exceptionally challenging and needed teamwork. I was physically fit, but obstacles like "Berlin Walls" or "Mud Mile" were designed to force racers to work with one another to complete the course. It didn't matter how fit you were. You needed help.

As entrepreneurs, we sometimes forget to ask for help. We should always be looking for help when and where it's needed.

Even if you could do everything on your own, you shouldn't. To avoid stunting the growth of your enterprise, you must empower a team that shares your vision. Two ideas are better than one, and a team-load of ideas can be revolutionary.

The old military management style of command-and-obey-without-question can be effective in our modern culture, but teams must be empowered with agreed-upon SMART goals (Specific, Measurable, Achievable, Relevant, and Time-bound), with regular meetings to discuss progress.

The obstacle ahead is simply that, an obstacle. The bridge is out, so build a bridge. Or fly over. What are the possibilities?

One of the main ways to keep an army from taking over a city is to take out the key areas of access. Specifically, the roads or bridges. The end of the movie Saving Private Ryan highlights this idea as the soldiers are trying hold the key bridge that could win or lose the war. It was so important that if the bridge was overrun, it was to be destroyed so the enemy could not utilize its access. Outnumbered and outgunned, only a handful of soldiers had to strategize and work together as a unit to defend the bridge.

As a teenager, I watched the U.S. military caravans canvasing the desert in Iraq. Humvees, tanks, and other vehicles were moving at top speed. But one vehicle stood out: the M60 (AVLB). AVLB stands for Armored Vehicle Launched Bridge, which is as specialized as you can imagine. Built on the chassis of the M60 tank, it's not designed for combat, but for deploying a sixty-foot bridge in just minutes, allowing troops and vehicles to cross otherwise impassable ravines. I was mesmerized to a wide crevasse so quickly bridged. No matter the danger, from crevasse to crevasse, they kept pressing forward.

Never let a danger sign say you can't make it until after you've creatively considered more options.

No matter the circumstance, look at the tools and resources around you. With a creative mind, ideas become the pathway to success. Are there helpful alternatives you hadn't seen until you took a closer look? Are there existing technologies or a new technology that could be created, something you never have considered before? Maybe they are co-workers. Friends, perhaps, both in personal and in business circles. Far too often, we miss winning the race just because we failed to look beyond our own abilities.

Escape Rooms

My first experience in an escape room was with the design team at Ardent Creative—an amazing way to support communication, imagination, and strategy. Each venture was different, posing different challenges and difficulties based on the people or the purpose.

We chose a medium difficulty room with a western theme. Our assigned guide monitored our progress and could give us three clues, if needed.

Our six-member team entered the small rectangular room with rough wood walls, a rustic old desk, and a few lanterns that provided minimal light. The guide went over the rules and time limits. The door behind us was locked, and we were given no way out until we used our clues and solved various riddles to open the door. Quickly, we noticed the three birds on the wall and looked at the various clues to escape. Slowly, we began to figure out how the process worked. Find the first clue, which led to another clue, and so on. We had to work together because each of us found different clues that had to be assembled to solve the puzzle. After fifteen minutes, we solved the final clue. The door unlocked.

Yeah, we completed the room and escaped. But wait, there was another room with more clues. How often does this happen in business? You solve one problem, get a big win, and wind up in another room with more problems to solve.

The next room reminded me of an old saloon. The large wooden table had a cash register and a locked box. On the walls hung various cuckoo clocks, each showing a different time. What did all this mean? After working through the first room, we better understood the process and quickly gathered clues. One after another, locks opened, and new clues were revealed. But wait! We faced a roadblock. Our guide seemed confused about a couple of clues, leaving us stuck with no way to proceed. We had solved one clue a step early, which the guide didn't realize until it was too late. With clarification and time added to the clock because of the mistake, we solved the final clue and entered the next room.

At this point, time was running out so we had to think quickly. This room looked like storage for explosives, with cables running across the floor. Under the pressing time constraints, we had to precisely communicate what each of us was seeing. I had never seen our team work so fast or communicate so clearly and effectively. We all knew the goal. Pressured, we worked creatively and quickly through the clues. In the end, we solved the final clue, blew up the TNT, and the last door opened. We had escaped with only seconds to spare.

Without every team member focusing on creatively

solving and communicating, the time would have expired, the game over when we'd barely started. Everyone had to contribute 100 percent effort to succeed. The practice in communication continued to help us as we focused on real problems under severe time constraints.

So what about a paper maze? A real-life maze and a paper maze are completely different. With a paper maze, you can see the whole thing before you, where the walls and boundaries are and how to navigate through. A leader, owner, or CEO should have a map of the maze. This could be a mission or vision, but the paper map is just a real map from 1,000 feet above. As leaders, you have to put yourself in position to see the path of the business from this perspective. This brings clarity and purpose you wouldn't otherwise have.

More than A-maze-ing

A rectangular maze puzzle typically enters on the left, winds through many turns while avoiding dead ends, and exits on the right. A circular maze often challenges us to find a way to the center. In every puzzle, the goal is the same: to get from where you are to where you want to be.

In business, we always navigate the maze with the destination in mind. Without a reward for finishing, there is no reason to start the game. We're always looking for a benefit greater than the cost.

In the movie *Inception*, the main character Cobb challenges Ariadne to draw a maze that he cannot solve in one minute. The first maze is simple—four-sided with horizontal and vertical lines, which Cobb stops her before the drawing was even finished and says, "Again." Challenged to do better, Ariadne adds complexity, with paths that look right until they reach a dead end. Cobb again stops her, grabs the paper, immediately solves the problem, and hands it back. "Going to have to do better than that." So far, Ariadne has shown her inability to meet the challenge. But she doesn't give up.

Frustrated, Ariadne realizes she must think outside the box. As her imaginations are stirred, she doesn't want the box. Instead, she draws an intricate and complex circular maze with no straight lines, where it was hard enough to know where to start, let alone how to finish.

Cobb couldn't solve the puzzle in and says, "That's more like it."

What's the point? Without a challenge, creativity and imagination are allowed to remain dormant. Necessity becomes the mother of invention. But let's be clear. For as long as we allow our employees to work inside their boxes, there will be no problem solving. First, we must clearly see the challenge. And then we must break into outside-the-box possibility thinking.

As in the *Inception* movie, imagination and pushing the envelope of thinking is the norm. We know to do that, but how? Without Cobb's challenge, Ariadne didn't have to think. At first, she didn't think creatively. But to meet the challenge, she had no choice.

Like Ariadne, we typically use the familiar until we realize that only the unfamiliar has any chance of working. What we had thought was good before must now change.

Cobb could quickly navigate a familiar maze structure. Once solved, that maze would never be a problem again. Knowing the path, of course you can immediately solve the puzzle.

What if I told you there are no rules to get to the end? What might you do differently? I didn't say you couldn't go over, under, or through any wall. In that case, you could simply draw a straight line from start to finish, and that would make the puzzle meaningless. Too easy. Okay, we can't go over, through, or beneath a wall. Besides that, you've tried every path and each one is a dead end. The problem can't be solved, can it? But wait! Nobody said you had to go forward from the start point. Let's go backward, move around the entire maze, and finish where we wanted to be.

What could you do differently to avoid the unavoidable pitfalls in business? Whatever you do must encourage people to be creative, because that's the only way they'll be ready to handle impossible situations.

Points to Ponder

- Avoid comfort zones: Familiar methods stifle creativity. Leaders must challenge teams to think outside the box, encouraging them to try unconventional problem-solving techniques.
- Be open to changing direction: Whether finding your way through a maze or discovering a solution to a business problem, flexibility is essential. Retrace your steps and think creatively about alternate solutions.
- Set high expectations: Without a challenge, creativity remains dormant. Every wall or barrier presents an opportunity for growth as teams step back and look at possibilities from different angles.

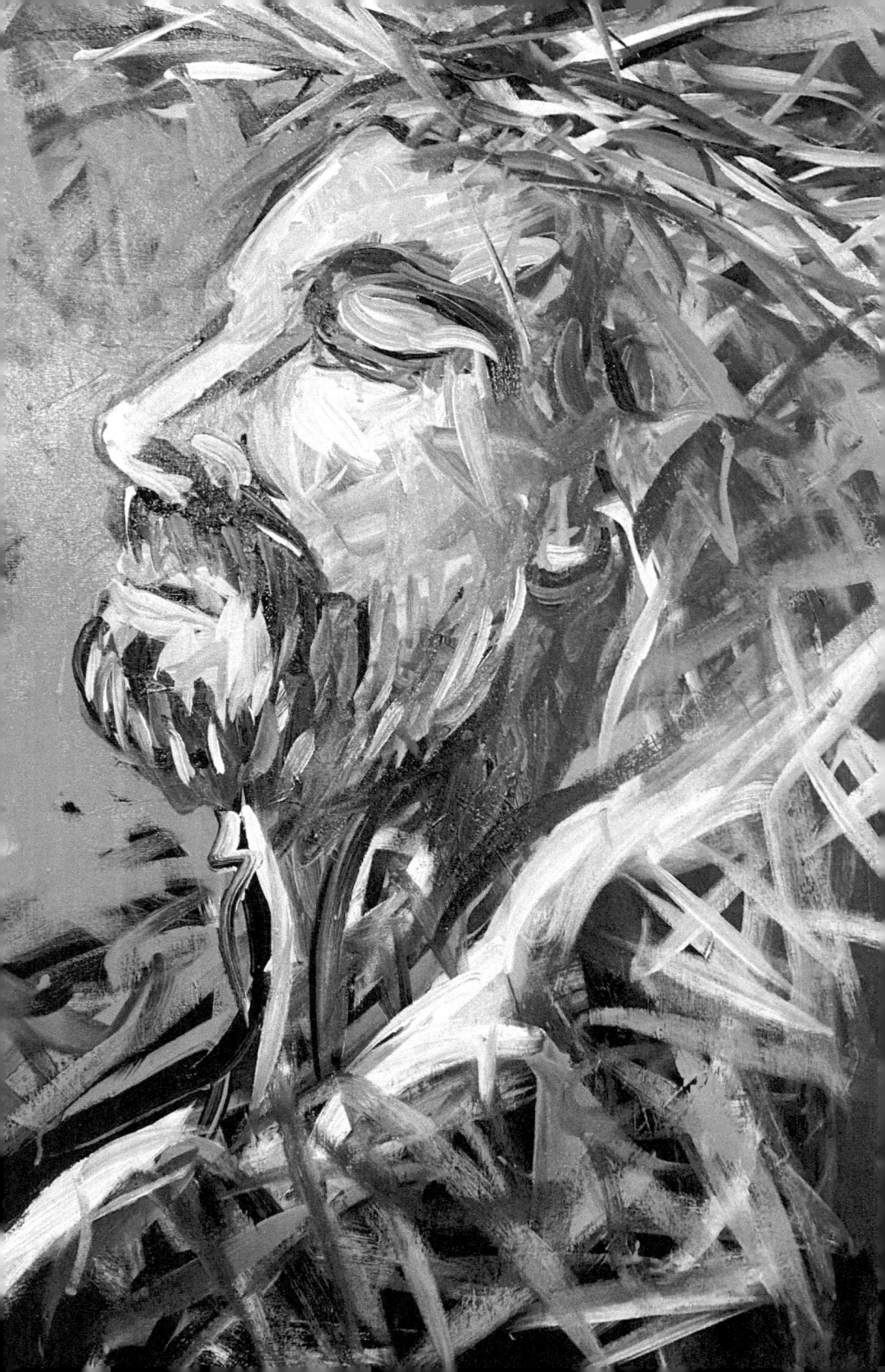

Your Final Masterpiece

Every work of art starts and ends with a brushstroke. While the work is not always easy, brushstroke after brushstroke, decision after decision, success or mistake leads to the end. A masterpiece!

As I reflect on the art of being an entrepreneur, I clearly see that this journey transcends the normal boundaries of business success. It is a personal odyssey, a creative endeavor that mirrors the complexities and beauties of life itself.

In all its craziness, your life is a masterpiece. Like the classic paintings of Vincent van Gogh, it is a canvas full of vibrant colors, bold strokes, and yes, many imperfections that give meaning to the trials and triumphs that are the true essence of the entrepreneurial spirit.

Your career is much more than a venture. It reflects your deepest values and aspirations. It stands as a testament to your creativity, resilience, and relentless pursuit of something greater than mere profit. It embodies your commitment to making a difference, to leaving an indelible mark on the world.

This is the art of entrepreneurship—a fusion of vision, passion, and purpose.

As you journey through the entrepreneurial landscape, remember that your greatest creation, your ultimate legacy, is not confined to the walls of your enterprise.

It extends to every aspect of your life, especially to those who walk this path with you—your family.

At home, far away from my business world, the Brad Ball family has its own mission and commitment statements that focus on love, faith, and community impact—a powerful reminder of what truly matters to us. I hope our family can be the guiding light in the night sky, showing a path that is about more than just a successful career.

Our Family Mission

Be a family that loves God, one another, and our neighbors as we make an impact in the world.

Our Commitment

Lead by example, showing the world what it means to be a family today. We are committed not only with one another but also with those around us, striving not to be afraid of risks and failure, never giving up.

Businesses often define their core values, but have you defined your *personal* values? In a core values exercise with Ray Sanders, I was given a deck of cards, each one with a different word. First, reviewed all the words and select the ten that were most important to me. This wasn't too hard, but then I had to remove five of the ten. I did this exercise twice, about a year a part. Not remembering what I did the first time, I went back through and selected five cards. Three were the same as before, and two were similar. My three key values were faith, legacy and integrity. Family/ love were similar. That choice was probably influenced by having my family with me. Wisdom had always been a big value, but the first time I didn't know there was a "write in" card, which meant I could add creativity.

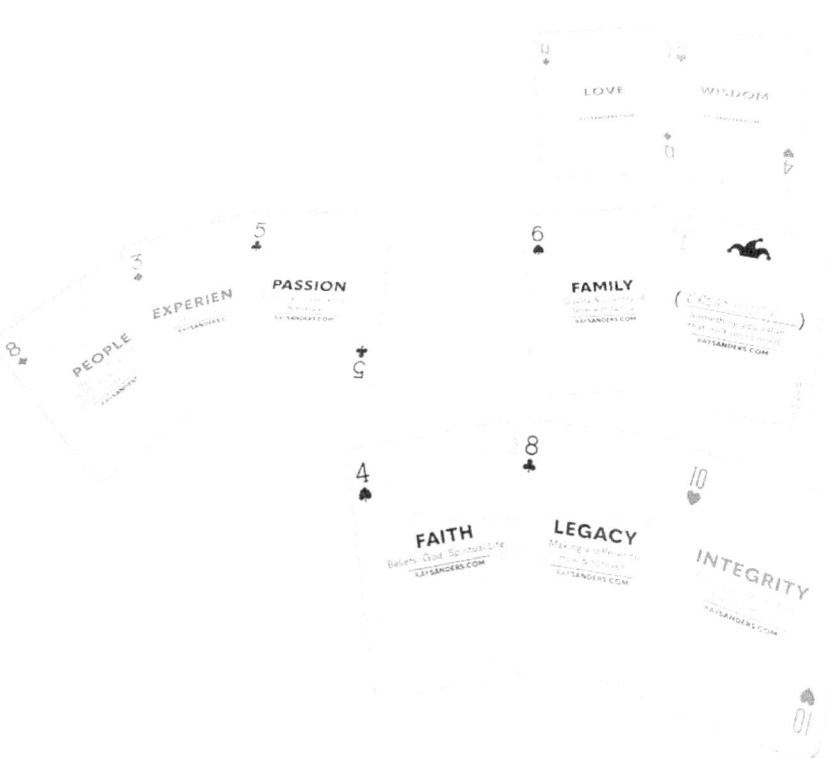

Why am I telling this story? Defining success by just money is a scary proposition. Money comes and goes, but do you really know what is most important to you? My five values define who I am, but legacy is the most important. That's because it's not defined by how much money I make but by the impact I leave on the lives around me. This includes my family, faith, and integrity, but it is also done through my creativity. This is my masterpiece.

The Artist's Masterpiece

It is settled, you are the masterpiece. When thinking about your entrepreneurial journey, consider the profound impact that your work has or will have upon your family, employees, and friends. How does will your entrepreneurial journey shape their perspectives, their values, and their dreams?

You must have a dream, the desire to fulfill that dream, and the determination to fulfill your Destiny. Dare to dream and envision your destiny. Reflect on the moments when your business taught resilience, about the importance of taking risks, learning new technology, and understanding the value of perseverance. Your venture is a living classroom, imparting lessons that extend far beyond the realms of commerce.

Your community is the broader canvas upon which your entrepreneurial brushstrokes leave a lasting impression. Think about how your business practices, the culture you foster, and the services or products you provide, which contribute to the society around you. Each decision you make and action you create ripples through the community, creating a legacy that can endure long after you've stepped away from day-to-day operations.

In this journey, remember that success is not solely measured by profit margins or market shares. It is also built upon quality relationships, the lives you touch, and the positive changes you encourage.

Your entrepreneurial endeavor is a powerful tool for social impact, a means to uplift, inspire, and transform.

At the crossroads of your entrepreneurial journey and personal legacy, take a moment to align your future pursuits with your core values and family mission. Envision a living, growing entity where your entrepreneurial story transforms your business from a mere profit center into a force for good, weaving your personal values into the fabric of your professional legacy.

The entrepreneurial journey is indeed a challenging one, filled with uncertainties and obstacles. But it is also a journey of incredible opportunity to grow, to learn, to innovate—to make meaningful contributions for the benefit of others. It is a journey that demands courage, creativity, and above all, a deep sense of worthwhile purpose.

So as you move forward in this journey, cherish each moment. Celebrate the successes, learn from the setbacks, and always focus on the bigger picture. Your entrepreneurial path is crafting a life that can be rich in meaning and purpose. Yes, it's about leaving a legacy that transcends commerce, touching the lives of those around you and shaping the world for future generations.

In the end, the true art of an entrepreneur lies not just in the wealth accumulated or the accolades received. It lies in the journey itself—in the experiences gained, the relationships nurtured, and the impact made.

This is the masterpiece you are creating, a masterpiece that is as unique and as extraordinary as you can be.

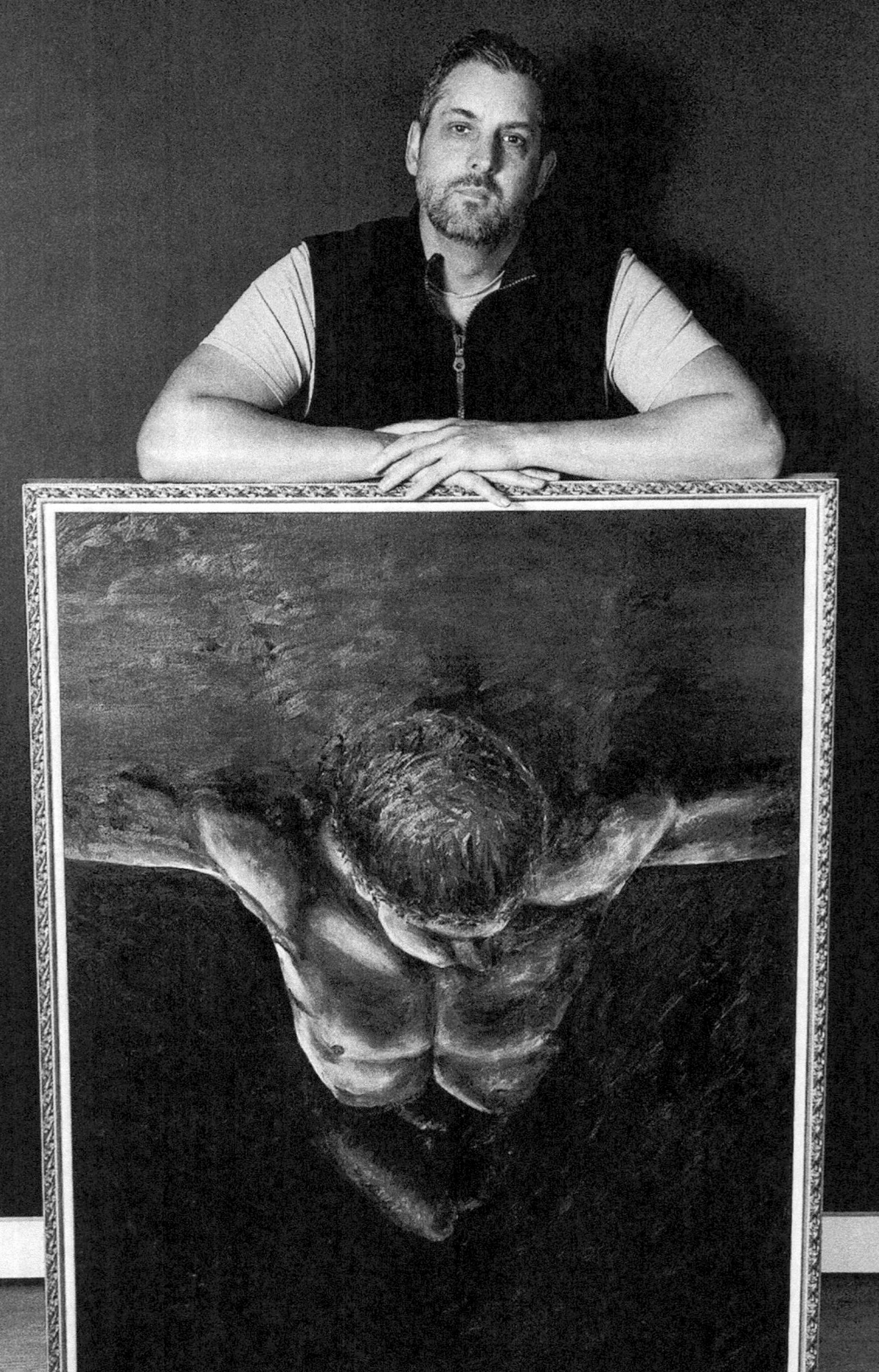

About the Author

Brad Ball is a dynamic entrepreneur and award-winning artist whose life and career are deeply intertwined with creativity. As the co-founder of Ardent Creative, a full-service agency specializing in design, development, marketing, and AI solutions, Brad has built a reputation for innovative problem-solving and visionary thinking. He is also a co-founder of Verity Software and a partner in the Committed Mastermind, where his expertise in business strategy and leadership continues to inspire others.

His unique fusion of art and business sets Brad apart. His live, on-stage performance art painting—a powerful expression of his creative spirit—has not only captivated audiences but has also opened doors in his entrepreneurial career. He firmly believes that creativity is the foundation of success, both in business and in everyday life. This belief, coupled with his view that nothing is by chance, has allowed him to channel the lessons learned from the canvas into the boardroom.

With over two decades of experience in the creative industry, he has consistently pushed the boundaries of what's possible when art meets entrepreneurship. His approach to business is as colorful and multifaceted as his paintings, always seeking new ways to blend innovation with practicality.

Brad's commitment to fostering creativity extends beyond his own work. He is passionate about nurturing the creative potential in others, whether it's his team at Ardent Creative, the entrepreneurs he mentors, or his own children. He believes that everyone has an inner artist waiting to be awakened, and that tapping into this creativity can lead to unprecedented success in any field.

Whether he is painting with a brush or shaping business strategies, Brad brings his bold, imaginative vision to everything he does. His clients benefit from this approach, as his artistry infuses each project with a distinctive blend of innovation and purpose. His work is a testament to the power of creativity in driving business success and personal fulfillment.

When not in the office or on stage, Brad can be found spending time with his family, sketching ideas in his ever-present notebook, or seeking new sources of inspiration in the world around him.

www.ingramcontent.com/pod-product-compliance
Lightning Source LLC
Chambersburg PA
CBHW060452290526
45791CB00001B/82